QUEEN MARGARET
OF SCOTLAND

Enjoy!.

Love. Sadie .

X.

First edition published by
NMSE Publishing
a division of NMS Enterprises Limited
National Museums of Scotland
Chambers Street
Edinburgh EHI IJF

This edition published by
NMS Enterprises Limited – Publishing
National Museums Scotland
Chambers Street
Edinburgh EHI IJF

British Library Cataloguing in Publication Data
A catalogue record for this book
is available from the British Library.

10 digit ISBN: 1 901663 92 2
13 digit ISBN: 978 1 901663 92 1

Cover design by Mark Blackadder.
Typesetting and internal layout by
NMS Enterprises Limited – Publishing.

The quotations in the text are from the undernoted sources:
The Anglo-Saxon Chronicle, trans. James Ingram (1823).
Lives of the Scottish Saints, trans. W. M. Metcalfe (1895).
William of Malmesbury's Chronicle of the Kings of England,
    trans. J. A. Giles (1847).
The New English Bible (1970).

QUEEN MARGARET
OF SCOTLAND

EILEEN DUNLOP

National Museums Scotland

The marriage of Queen Margaret to Malcolm Canmore in Dunfermline Abbey, 1070.
etching by Alexander Runciman (c.1771). From a volume in the library of National
Museums Scotland containing works presented to the Society of Antiquaries of
Scotland by various donors. Reproduced by permission of NMS Library (© Trustees
of the National Museums of Scotland).

For Ena, Jamie and Deirdre

CONTENTS

Acknowledgements   ix

The Ancestry of Queen Margaret   x

The Kings of Scotland 1005-1153   xi

Europe A.D. c.1050   xii

The British Isles A.D. c.1050   xiii

1   Images of Margaret   1

2   Unruly Times   8

3   A Hungarian Childhood   15

4   English Influences   23

5   Conquest   31

6   The King of Scots   38

7   Court and Country   45

8   Margaret's Church   55

9   The Queen's Brother   64

10   Last Days   72

11   The Legacy of Margaret   81

12   The Making of a Saint   89

Bibliography   99

Places to Visit   103

Index   105

Queen Margaret and King Malcolm (1887): oil painting by Sir Joseph Noel Paton (1821-1902). Reproduced by permission of the Dunfermline Carnegie Trust.

ACKNOWLEDGEMENTS

I AM indebted to many people for help, encouragement and advice in the writing of this book. They have answered questions, lent me books, sent me articles and generously put me in touch one with another. I am particularly grateful to the following: Professor A. A. M. Duncan, Dr Donal Bateson (Hunterian Museum, Glasgow University), Dr David Caldwell (National Museums of Scotland), Dairmid Gunn, Alastair Cherry, Walter Awlson, Roberta Meek, Connie Brodie, George Robertson, Jean Lewis and Eileen Crerar-Gilbert. I am indebted to Andrew R. Nicoll of the Scottish Catholic Archives for giving me access to papers relating to Bishop James Gillis, and I wish to acknowledge the research of Wendy J. Sinclair in helping me to an understanding of Queen Margaret's complicated maternal lineage. Special thanks are due to Dr Bob Cowan and to Peter Hennessy, my advisers on medical and spiritual matters, to my publisher Lesley A. Taylor and my editor Cara Shanley and reader Iseabail Macleod. Finally, heartfelt gratitude to my husband, Antony Kamm, who has listened patiently for two years to talk of Queen Margaret, dealt calmly with my frequent computer crises, compiled the index and provided a fund of support, enthusiasm and helpful advice.

Eileen Dunlop

THE ANCESTRY OF QUEEN MARGARET

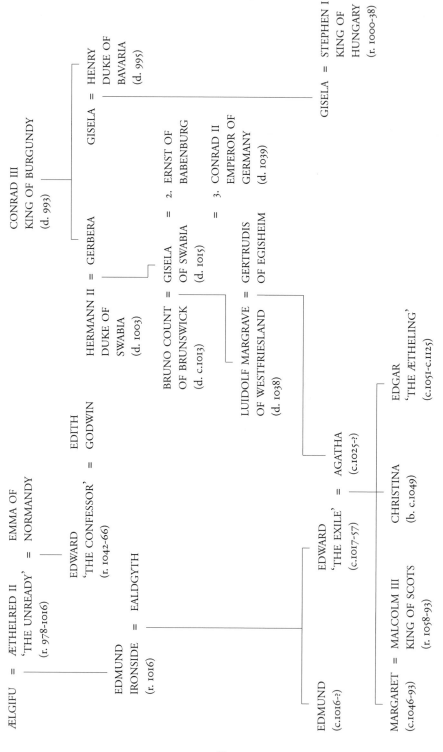

ÆLGIFU = ÆTHELRED II 'THE UNREADY' (r. 978–1016)

EMMA OF NORMANDY

EDWARD 'THE CONFESSOR' (r. 1042–66) = EDITH

GODWIN

EDMUND IRONSIDE = EALDGYTH (r. 1016)

CONRAD III KING OF BURGUNDY (d. 993)

GISELA = HENRY DUKE OF BAVARIA (d. 995)

GERBERA = HERMANN II DUKE OF SWABIA (d. 1003)

BRUNO COUNT OF BRUNSWICK (d. c.1013) = GISELA OF SWABIA (d. 1015)

2. ERNST OF BABENBURG

3. CONRAD II EMPEROR OF GERMANY (d. 1039)

LUIDOLF MARGRAVE OF WESTFRIESLAND (d. 1038) = GERTRUDIS OF EGISHEIM

GISELA = STEPHEN I KING OF HUNGARY (r. 1000–38)

EDWARD 'THE EXILE' (c.1017–57) = AGATHA (c.1025–?)

EDMUND (c.1016–?)

EDGAR 'THE ÆTHELING' (c.1051–c.1125)

CHRISTINA (b. c.1049)

MARGARET = MALCOLM III KING OF SCOTS (c.1046–93) (r. 1058–93)

x

THE KINGS OF SCOTLAND 1005-1153

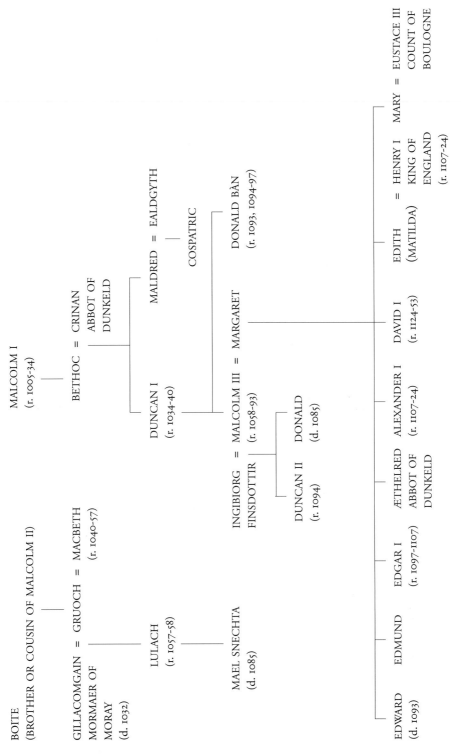

EUROPE A.D. c.1050

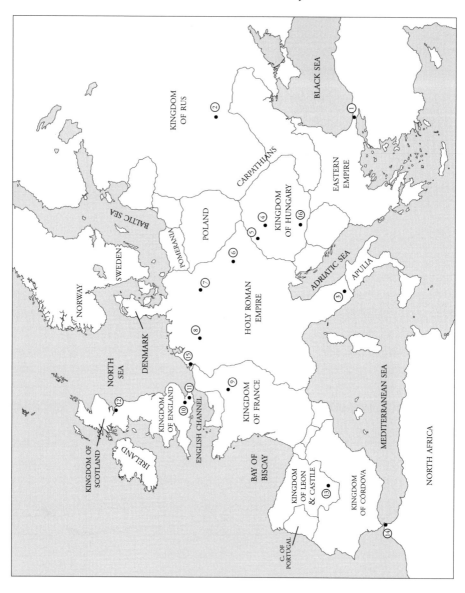

EUROPE A.D. c.1050
1. Constantinople
2. Kiev
3. Rome
4. Esztergom
5. Pressburg
6. Prague
7. Cologne
8. Magdeburg
9. Paris
10. London
11. Canterbury
12. Edinburgh
13. Madrid
14. Tangier
15. Antwerp
16. Pècs

THE BRITISH ISLES A.D. c.1050
1. Scone
2. St Andrews
3. Dunfermline
4. Edinburgh
5. Berwick-upon-Tweed
6. Alnwick
7. Tynemouth
8. Newcastle
9. Durham
10. Carlisle
11. York
12. Gloucester
13. Oxford
14. Wilton
15. Salisbury
16. Winchester
17. London
18. Canterbury
19. Dover
20. Hastings
21. Dunkerque
22. Boulogne
23. St Valery
24. Quentovic
25. Dublin
26. Iona

THE BRITISH ISLES A.D. c.1050

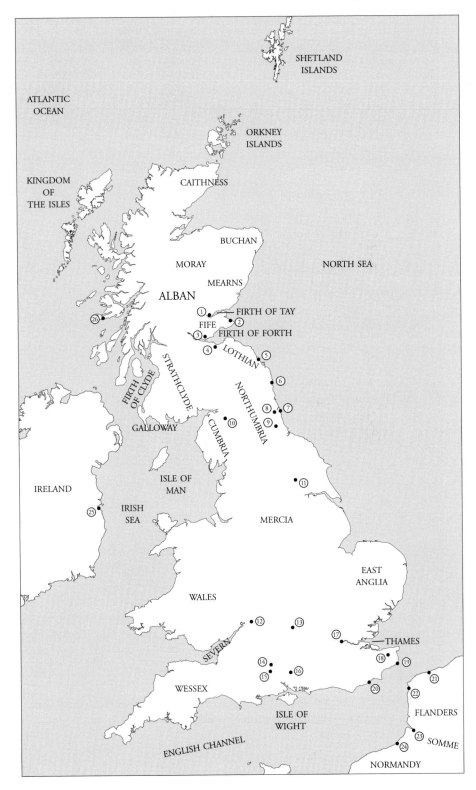

ATLANTIC
OCEAN

SHETLAND
ISLANDS

ORKNEY
ISLANDS

KINGDOM
OF
THE ISLES

CAITHNESS

BUCHAN

MORAY

NORTH SEA

MEARNS

ALBAN

① ── FIRTH OF TAY
FIFE ②
③ FIRTH OF FORTH
④ LOTHIAN ⑤

FIRTH
OF CLYDE

STRATHCLYDE

NORTHUMBRIA

⑥

GALLOWAY

CUMBRIA

⑧ ⑦
⑨

⑩

⑪

ISLE OF
MAN

IRELAND

IRISH
SEA

㉕

㉖

MERCIA

EAST
ANGLIA

WALES

⑫ ⑬

⑰ ── THAMES
⑱ ⑲

SEVERN

⑭ ⑯
⑮

⑳

㉑

㉒

WESSEX

ISLE OF
WIGHT

FLANDERS

㉓ SOMME

㉔

ENGLISH CHANNEL

NORMANDY

The Landing of St Margaret at Queensferry: frieze (detail) by William Hole (fl.1873-93). Reproduced by permission of the Scottish National Portrait Gallery.

I

IMAGES
OF MARGARET

I N 1785, six hundred and ninety-two years after the death of Queen
Margaret of Scotland, a young priest named James Carruthers was paying
a visit to his old school. The seminary at Douai, near Lille in north-east France,
was one of several 'Scots Colleges' on the continent of Europe, forced abroad
by the upheaval of the Scottish Reformation in the sixteenth and early seventeenth centuries. As well as continuing to educate young Scots for the Roman
Catholic priesthood, it had quickly become a safe repository for treasures
endangered by the iconoclasm sweeping Scotland as the new religion dis-
placed the old. While in residence, James Carruthers witnessed a macabre but
fascinating event – and, naturally for a man who was later to become a prolific
historian, carefully recorded what he had seen.

Among the precious relics deposited for safe keeping in the church of the
Scots College was a thirteenth-century head shrine, known to contain the
embalmed head of Margaret of Scotland, queen and saint. In 1695 it had been
described by Father Stephen Maxwell, Rector of the College as 'a bust … not
only larger than life and entirely of silver, but also, in the crown and in the
collar that overspreads the breast, rich with gems and pearls'. Venerated before
the Reformation by pilgrims to the shrine of St Margaret at Dunfermline,
this priceless object had since travelled far. Once in the care of Mary, queen
of Scots in Edinburgh Castle, it had in 1587 emerged from a period of conceal-
ment at Craigluscar in Fife to be taken by a missionary Jesuit to Antwerp,
and thence thirty years later to Douai. It was on St Margaret's feast day, 10
June 1785, that James Carruthers saw the head shrine opened and the contents
revealed. The saint's head, he noted, was 'in extraordinary preservation, with
a quantity of hair, fair in colour, still upon it'. Since four years later, in a
further orgy of iconoclasm fuelled by the French Revolution, the head shrine
disappeared from history, Carruthers's witness statement provides the only
reliable clue we have to the physical appearance of Queen Margaret.

This is worth noting because representations of the queen are so numerous, and so misleading. Margaret's iconic status was long unquestioned in Scotland. As late as 2000, in a poll conducted by *The Scottish Review* to identify 'the greatest Scot in history', she was the highest placed woman, despite not having a drop of Scottish blood in her veins. Even before her canonisation in 1249 she was a cult figure, so it is not surprising that by the fifteenth century she was appearing, conventionally haloed, in illuminated manuscripts such as Robert Blackadder's prayer-book (c.1490). Thereafter there were numerous attempts to depict her, more interesting for what they tell us about the times in which they were created than for the light they shed on their subject. In the Seton Armorial, a book of heraldry commissioned by the 5th Lord Seton and illustrated (c.1580) by an unknown artist, Margaret and her husband, King Malcolm III of Scots, stand stiffly resplendent in the fashionable clothes of the Stewart court. At the Scots College at Salamanca in Spain, there is a painting of Margaret, dark-haired, ecstatic, crowned and attired in the height of mid-seventeenth century fashion. Not until the eighteenth century do we find a genuine attempt to evoke a bygone age; an etching of the marriage of Margaret and Malcolm III shows new imaginative boldness. For all its intense dramatic atmosphere, however, its presentation of period costume, both regal and clerical, is entertainingly wide of the mark.

The nineteenth century brought a much greater concern for historical veracity but, paradoxically, the images feed most powerfully the legend rather than the reality of Margaret. In a well-known depiction in the Scottish National Portrait Gallery by William Hole (fl.1873-93), a beautifully dressed and demure princess is seen first setting foot in Scotland from a richly ornamented longship. Carefully researched, lovingly detailed and decorative in the high Victorian style, it was a favourite illustration in children's history books until well into the twentieth century. An almost equally famous painting is by the Dunfermline-born Sir Joseph Noel Paton (1821-1902), which was bequeathed to the Dunfermline Carnegie Trust. Dated 1887, it shows clearly Paton's link, through his lifelong friendship with Sir John Everett Millais, to the English Pre-Raphaelite ideals. The scene is set in an exquisitely detailed wooded glade, where a rapt, flowing-haired Margaret is reading the Gospel to her pensive, illiterate and fully-armed husband. There is a meticulous striving for authenticity in dress and ornament, but the work is more like an illustration for Tennyson's Arthurian *Idylls of the King* than a portrait of real eleventh-century people. Nonetheless, like the painting by William Hole, it has informed our perception of Queen Margaret. When we think of her, these are among the images that come to mind.

Following the trend of twentieth-century art, recent portrayals of Margaret have been more austere. The most famous of all, however, stands on the borderline between romanticism and modern form. Seen each year by thousands of visitors to the tiny twelfth-century oratory in Edinburgh Castle known as 'St Margaret's Chapel', it is not a painting but a work in stained glass. Made by the Scottish artist Douglas Strachan (1875-1950) and gifted by him when the chapel was restored in 1934, it fills one of four window spaces. Unlike much ecclesiastical stained glass which overwhelms by its size and variety, Strachan's presentation of Margaret works through the beauty of its colour and its strange double sense of intimacy and distance. Transcending historical accuracy, it draws poignantly on the ancient, tender legend of the saintly young woman who yearned to be a nun but accepted that it was her destiny to be a queen. Beneath the coat of arms said to have been conferred on her by Edward the Confessor, Margaret stands with her famous Gospel book open in her hands. All the traditional features are present – the golden crown, the richly glowing robe and beautifully braided hair – but it is the face that haunts the imagination. Young, regal, resolute and, in the poet Charles Causley's phrase, 'as cool as history', this Margaret is both benign and aloof, challenging the observer while giving little of herself away. Devoid of any sense of inner turmoil or the violence of the period in which her life was set, this portrait more than any other embodies the serene and saintly figure whom generations of Scots have loved and revered. Yet it too is only one artist's impression of a woman who died in 1093; all we know for certain is that in 1785 she was observed to have had fair hair.

Turning to the written sources of Margaret's life, we find more that is of ancient provenance, but here too some caution is in order. The resources of modern biographers are not available in writing about someone who lived so long ago; there are no letters or diaries to give insight into the inner mind. Other writings from Margaret's period are sparse by modern standards; apart from two chronicles compiled in the twelfth century and associated with the monasteries of Holyrood and Melrose, there is no Scottish record available until *Chronica gentis Scotorum*, the chronicle of the Scottish people, composed by the Aberdeen cleric John of Fordun (c.1320-64). John's work, which is the basis of the first part of the *Scotichronicon*, the great sourcebook of Scottish history amplified and completed by Walter Bower (1383-1437), was undertaken in the aftermath of the bitter wars with England over Scottish independence. Although John was motivated by the tragic destruction of the written records of Scotland after the wars, he did have access to other documents since lost, and his work is of great scholarly importance. Unfortunately, since he began his account with the biblical flood and many of his more recent sources were scarcely more credible, as history it is not very reliable.

For a contemporary record of Margaret's period, we have to turn to the great English chroniclers of the eleventh century – monks such as Symeon of Durham, William of Malmesbury, Florence of Worcester and Joscelin of Canterbury – and to the compilers and scribes of the great *Anglo-Saxon Chronicle*. There is considerable mention of Scottish kings and Scottish affairs in these accounts, which are illuminating provided that certain points are kept in mind. First, that the chroniclers were writing their own national story, and had no interest in the Scots except as they impinged on English affairs. Second that, confined to their monasteries, dependent on indifferent written sources and a lot of gossip, they frequently contradicted each other. Third, that they were prejudiced against the Scots, genuinely believing them to be barbarous; the behaviour of the Scots during repeated raids into Northumbria, which included burning churches and even ravaging the Holy Island of Lindisfarne, had not endeared them to monks like Symeon of Durham, or to his contacts on the monastic grapevine. Moreover, although the chroniclers noted Margaret's exalted lineage, piety and good works, she was only a minor figure in their record. They saw her as her brother's sister and her husband's wife, and she does not owe her iconic status in Scotland to them.

As recently as thirty years ago, every primary school pupil in Scotland learned that Margaret was a beautiful English princess who, escaping from the wicked king William the Conqueror, was driven by a storm into the estuary of the River Forth. Here the good king of Scots rescued her, fell in love and married her, and together they had six sons and two daughters. Children also learned that Queen Margaret built a church at Dunfermline, fed orphans and gave generously to the poor – and that, shocked by the heretical practices of the native church, the primitive facilities at court and the loutish manners of the Scots, she introduced 'civilising' reforms in both church and state. This familiar account, once accepted meekly but nowadays the source of much indignation, is drawn almost entirely from one source, *Vita Sanctae Margaretae*, the 'Life of St Margaret' written by 'T, a servant of the servants of St Cuthbert', meaning a monk of Durham. The original is long lost, but the text still exists in three variant manuscripts dating from the thirteenth century. There has been scholarly debate over the date of writing and the authorship, but it is now generally accepted that the *Life* was written between

1100 and 1110 by Turgot, an ecclesiastic of some distinction who claimed to have known Margaret from her youth, and to have been her confidant and confessor.

Born in Lincolnshire during the reign of Cnut, Turgot was probably of Danish descent. After the Norman Conquest of 1066, he spent a period of exile in Norway, where he is said to have taught psalmody to King Olaf, the son of Harald Hardrada. Returning to England, he became a Benedictine monk at Jarrow and, in 1087, was appointed prior of Durham. It is unlikely that he was ever more than an occasional visitor to the court of Malcolm III although, when he came to write his memoir of Margaret, he clearly had intimate knowledge both of his subject and of the royal household. Turgot's narrative has often been praised for its simple style and for his reluctance to rely on the miraculous. He said,

> *Let others admire the tokens of miracles which they see in others. I, for my part, admire much more the works of mercy which I saw in Margaret. Miracles are common to the evil and to the good, but the works of true piety and charity belong to the good alone.*

Until comparatively recently, this apparently reasonable and moderate stance led to the account being accepted more or less at face value.

By the middle of the twentieth century, however, the tide was turning against Turgot. Modern scholars have been critical, castigating his mental vagueness, rhetorical mannerisms and lack of interest in topography. The fairy tale aspects of his narrative have been ridiculed and, in a changed political and religious climate, Scots' indignation at his portrayal of their forebears has taken the place of reverence for his subject. In some quarters, Margaret has become less a saint than an interfering English busybody, bent on obliterating Scots identity and destroying a thriving, if idiosyncratic, Scottish church. Yet Turgot's *Life* is the bedrock of our knowledge of Margaret; without it there would be little to believe or disbelieve. Some understanding of the circumstances and literary conventions of its writing is therefore needed, in order to form a balanced view of the writer and of Margaret herself.

Turgot, from his own account, was writing in response to an important act of patronage. Margaret's elder daughter Matilda, who in 1100 had become queen of England, had invited him to write a memoir of her mother, trusting him because 'by reason of [his] great friendship with [Margaret]' he was 'in great part familiar with her secret thoughts'. Matilda, who in Scotland had been called Edith, had been sent away to school as a small child and, sadly, had little recollection of her mother. Turgot was no doubt flattered by Matilda's invitation, and intended some flattery in return. That he also anticipated a wider English readership is clear from his emphasis on Margaret's English descent and liking for things Norman; the marriage of Matilda and Henry I, youngest son of William the Conqueror, was widely seen as a reconciliation between the Normans and the old Anglo-Saxon dynasty to which Margaret belonged.

The form Turgot chose was hagiography, a reverent and idealising genre which had its own conventions in medieval times, one being that readers were attuned to the difference between literal and spiritual truth. As pointed out fifty years ago by the historian R. L. G. Ritchie, hagiography's sole purpose was to emphasise the sanctity of its subject, to pump up his or her importance at the expense of everyone and everything else. On this reading, Turgot's partisan description was intended simply to enhance the importance of 'his' saint and his disparagement of Malcolm III's power, majesty and intellectual ability, and of the Scots generally, was not intended to offend. Modern Scots' bristling at Turgot's unfortunately vivid description of Malcolm and his uncivilised court arises, therefore, from ignorance of the genre and misunderstanding of authorial intention.

Which is all very well, up to a point. It is worth remembering, however, that Turgot did not come unprejudiced to his task. Like Symeon the chronicler, he was a monk of Durham who knew all about the atrocities committed in Northumbria by Scottish raiders, with King Malcolm at their head. Moreover, Turgot had in 1074 had a personal encounter with Malcolm which must have hurt his dignity and left a bitter taste in his mouth. With Aldwin, a fellow monk from Jarrow, and on the authority of Walcher, the Norman bishop of Durham, Turgot had attempted to plant a Benedictine monastery at Melrose, which was within the civil jurisdiction of Scotland. Although Melrose, with good enough historical reason, was claimed ecclesiastically by the see of Durham, Malcolm saw this settlement as challenging the authority of the Celtic bishop of St Andrews as well as his own. When Aldwin and Turgot refused to swear fealty to him, he smashed up their monastery and chased them back over the border. It is hard to believe that, when Turgot came to write his account of Margaret's life, time had erased the memory of this humiliation, and that his depiction of the Scots king has no element of revenge.

So if every likeness of Queen Margaret is imaginary and all the primary sources are, by modern standards, either dubious or prejudiced, is it possible to form a more balanced view of a woman who still provokes and disturbs? The answer is that it ought to be, because we are no longer entirely dependent on the primary sources. Ever since the publication of W. F. Skene's *Celtic Scotland: A History of Ancient Alban* between 1886 and 1890, the history of eleventh-century Scotland has been subjected to rigorous examination by scholars and archaeologists. This must frequently have been a frustrating task, since many documents perished during the centuries of war, and the climate has not been kind to the fabric of the past. Next to nothing remains of buildings, clothing and ornament; even St Margaret's Chapel is now known to post-date her lifetime, while the stone remnant of her shrine at Dunfermline gives no clue to its ancient superstructure. Research has, however, produced convincing reconstructions of the period and a much more coherent picture of politics, personalities and international relations has emerged. Preconceptions of a backward, marginalised country have been challenged, and a scrupulous effort has been made to separate the facts from the myth – although in Scotland the power of myth should never be underestimated.

Margaret's position in the borderland of legend and history is entirely due to Turgot. It was he who set her on a pinnacle of perfection from which, in our ironic and iconoclastic age, she was bound to fall. Yet even his detractors admit that he knew his subject, and the fact that his *Life* is full of pious overstatement should not obscure its substratum of truth. We shall never know what Margaret really looked like, or what finally happened to her remains. Her personality and motives will remain contentious, and there are blanks in her story that can only speculatively be filled. But, from ancient sources modified by modern scholarship, it is possible to chart her life, and to understand why she made such a lasting impression on the country to which she came as a refugee more than nine centuries ago.

2

UNRULY TIMES

S COTLAND was not the only country where Margaret lived as a foreigner to claim her as one of its own. Images of her can be seen in churches throughout Hungary, and in the cathedral of Esztergom, the ancient capital, there is a notice stating that she was the granddaughter of St Stephen, who ruled as king in Hungary from 1000 until 1038. This is untrue, but the unqualified public statement suggests that Margaret's legend thrives as well in Hungary as in Scotland. To understand why Margaret was possibly born and certainly reared in Hungary, it is helpful to know something of her family's background and to trace the adventurous life of her father, Edward, sometimes known as 'the Exile'. Edward was born c.1017 in England, the son and grandson of kings who claimed descent from Cerdic, the semi-mythical Saxon said to have landed in Hampshire in 495. Cerdic was credited with the creation of the kingdom of Wessex and with the foundation of the West Saxon dynasty which, with minor interruptions, endured until the Norman Conquest.

Because Turgot makes Margaret such a serene figure, confined in a little world of church, good works and domestic affairs, it is easy to forget what a tumultuous century she lived in. Her immediate ancestors on the English side had been deeply involved in warfare and political strife, sometimes leading to open murder and sometimes to death too convenient to be unsuspicious. Her great-grandfather, Æthelred II 'the Unready' or 'the Ill-advised', had become king in circumstances that scandalised even an age largely inured to violence. In 978 his elder half-brother King Edward, subsequently known as 'the Martyr', was paying a friendly visit to Æthelred and his mother at Corfe Castle in Dorset when he was brutally attacked and murdered. It is known that the thirteen year-old Æthelred's mother planned and perhaps even participated in this wicked betrayal of hospitality in order to put him on the throne, although apparently poor Æthelred had no such ambition. It is said that when he realised what had been done, he howled and sobbed so inconsolably that his mother lost her temper and beat him with a candlestick.

Possibly Æthelred was prescient. From this grim start, his long reign deteriorated into a spasmodic but bloody struggle against the Scandinavian invaders known as Vikings or Danes, whose cruel attacks had already been a hazard of English life for two centuries. After early attempts to buy the enemy off, Æthelred lost patience and, in 1002, ordered a massacre of Danes who had settled in the north of England – a rash act which provoked a devastating response from Swein Forkbeard, king of Denmark, and his son Cnut. The remaining fourteen years of Æthelred's reign were scarred by wave upon wave of bloodthirsty attacks which he was unable to repel, less perhaps because he was badly advised than because of the greater strength and determination of the Danes. In 1013 he was forced to flee to Normandy, leaving Swein in possession of the whole country and, although he was reprieved and unenthusiastically reinstated when Swein died a year later, his troubles were far from over. His eldest son Æthelstan died prematurely and his son-in-law Eadric Streona, whom he had made ealdorman or sub-ruler of Mercia and to whom he entrusted state secrets, betrayed him by defecting to Cnut. In 1016 Æthelred died in London, as yet another fleet of Danish longships was heading towards the Thames.

After such a troubled life, it is perhaps surprising that Margaret's great-grandfather lived into his fifties and died in his bed. Her grandfather was not destined to live so long, and his end was equivocal. The death of Æthelstan had left as Æthelred's heir his second son Edmund, 'called Ironside,' according to the *Anglo-Saxon Chronicle*, 'because of his valour'. Edmund had already shown his determination to stamp his authority on England, challenging both the power and the influence of the uppity Eadric. In 1015, when Æthelred was seriously losing his grip on affairs, two other noblemen whom he trusted, Sigeferth and Morcar, had been murdered at Oxford on Eadric's orders. Edmund acted decisively; snatching Sigeferth's widow, Ealdgyth ('a woman,' notes the chronicler William of Malmesbury, 'remarkable for her rank and beauty', of whom Edmund 'became enamoured') from Eadric's custody, he promptly married her. At the same time, says the *Chronicle*, 'he took possession of all Sigeferth's estates, and Morcar's, and the people submitted to him'. Whether Margaret's grandmother was 'enamoured', and how she felt about the peremptoriness of her second marriage are not recorded; in any event, although greatly significant in the context of Margaret's story, it was not destined to last long. On his father's death Edmund was proclaimed king in

London, but a few days later in Southampton a larger assembly swore fealty to Cnut. A heroic and often evenly balanced campaign followed, but the end was inevitable. In October 1016 Edmund, again betrayed by the odious Eadric, was crushingly defeated at Assandûn (Ashingdon in Essex) by Cnut.

Cnut was a pragmatic man and, in the aftermath of this decisive battle, he decided to talk peace. Meeting Edmund at Olney in Gloucestershire, he agreed with him a division of authority in England. Six weeks later, however, Edmund was dead. It is possible, although he was not much over thirty, that he was already ill and died from natural causes, but the convenience of his death to Cnut, who now took control of the whole country, of course provoked dark rumour. William of Malmesbury, in a deliciously gossipy passage, admits that there is no absolute proof concerning the 'mischance' that caused Edmund's death, then proceeds, gleefully and memorably, to record what 'fame asperses'. Unsurprisingly, Eadric was again involved. Acting 'through regard for Cnut', he discovered that

> there were two attendants on the king to whom he had committed the entire care of his person and ... seducing them by promises, at length made them his accomplices. At his suggestion, they drove an iron hook into [Edmund's] posteriors, as he was sitting down for a necessary purpose.

It is satisfying to note that Cnut's regard for Eadric was no less cynical; within a year he had piously denounced him as a traitor to King Edmund. Eadric was strangled in Cnut's presence, then pitched unceremoniously through a window into the River Thames.

From his brief marriage with Ealdgyth, Edmund Ironside left two infants, the younger of whom would become Margaret's father. It has been suggested that, since their parents had been married only fifteen months, these boys, Edmund and Edward, must have been twins; it is more probable that the younger was born posthumously. It is known that, thirty years later, they were alive and living in Hungary, but how they got there has long been a subject of dispute and speculation.

Clearly the existence of Anglo-Saxon male heirs proved a problem for Cnut because of the likelihood that, as they grew up, they would become the focus of malcontents among the nobility. To the chroniclers, therefore, Cnut was the obvious villain of the piece. According to William of Malmesbury, he despatched the two boys to his half-brother King Olaf of Sweden to be murdered. This is not impossible, since Cnut represented the great paradox of early kingship, the devout, observant Christian who was capable of the cruellest acts to secure his temporal power. King Olaf, continues William, could not bring himself to do the deed because *he* was a Christian, but it seems just as likely that he declined to do Cnut's dirty work since the boys were no threat to him. In another version, penned in the twelfth century by a Norman, Geoffrei Gaimar, the children remained in England until they were twelve, when Cnut's second wife, Emma of Normandy, persuaded him to engineer their disappearance so that the sons of her first marriage might inherit. This is improbable, because by 1028 Emma had a son with Cnut, Harthacnut, whom she clearly favoured. According to this version, one Earl Walgar was detailed to get rid of Edmund Ironside's children, but instead abandoned his estates and fled with them to Denmark.

At this point, the confusion and contradictions of the story have barely begun. The early medieval chroniclers present seriously conflicting versions of the journey from Scandinavia to Hungary, dates given do not correspond to known events and, since there is no mention in extant Hungarian sources of the princes' residence there, for many years it seemed that fact might never be disentangled from fancy and romance. Only recently, through the patient research of Scottish scholars, notably Professor G. W. S. Barrow, Wendy J. Sinclair and Alan J. Wilson, has a coherent narrative at last emerged. It is not agreed by all, and may in future be challenged by new information, but since it transcends the troubling inconsistencies of other versions, I have made it the basis of the following account.

Soon after their father's death, the tiny princes were placed in the charge of the Danish earl Walgar, who had orders quietly to get rid of them. (What happened to Ealdgyth is unknown, although she too probably went into exile.) Earl Walgar, whose private intention remains obscure, took the babies to Sweden where, King Olaf being disinclined to infanticide, they remained under his protection. Interestingly, they seem to have disappeared from English consciousness for almost forty years, since even after the extinction of Cnut's bloodline in 1042 their claim to the succession was ignored. This suggests that Cnut believed that they were dead, and that his friends shared his view. In 1022 King Olaf died, leaving three children, Prince Anund Jakob, who succeeded him, and two daughters. One, Astrid, was married to King Olaf II of Norway, the other, Ingegerd, to Jaraslow I, Great Prince of Kiev. Since Ingegerd seems also to have been a half-sister of their mother Ealdgyth, these alliances would be vital to the sons of Edmund Ironside.

In 1028, when the boys were twelve and eleven, Cnut invaded Norway, causing King Olaf II and his son Magnus to flee to Sweden, *en route* to Russia. With Cnut on the rampage and so uncomfortably close, it was decided that Edmund and Edward would be safer away from Sweden. With Olaf and Magnus, they travelled south to the court of Prince Jaraslow at Kiev. There was a strong connection between Kiev and Scandinavia; the city had been founded in the late eighth century by the famous Rurik, one of many Norse pirates who plundered the length of the rivers between the Baltic and the Caspian seas. Situated at the confluence of the Dneiper and several tributaries, Kiev quickly developed as the hub of trading routes from north to south and east to west. The descendants of Rurik grew wealthy; as well as Kiev they ruled Novgorod and Moscow until the end of the sixteenth century. Prince Jaraslow was famously sympathetic to royal exiles, and it is reasonable to suppose that the young princes were doubly welcome on account of their relationship with Princess Ingegerd and their adoption by the Swedish royal house. It has been suggested that they may also have spent time further north, on the estate at Gardrike, on Lake Lagoda, which their aunt Ingegerd had received from her husband as a wedding present. Certainly their years under the protection of Prince Jaraslow were the longest and most settled period of their turbulent early life.

Around 1037, when Edmund and Edward were just over twenty, two other young princes arrived at the hospitable court of Kiev. They were Andrew (András) and Levente, the two elder sons of Vászoly, cousin of King (St) Stephen I of Hungary. After the death of his only surviving son in 1031, Stephen had named Vászoly as his heir, but had come to believe that Vászoly, while paying lip-service to Christianity, was privately worshipping pagan gods. Relations between king and heir broke down; Stephen withdrew his pledge of succession to Vászoly and, in another act which sits uneasily with our modern notion of Christian behaviour, had his eyes gouged out and his ears filled with molten lead. Vászoly's sons, who also had a family connection with Jaraslow, fled to him. It would have been strange if no bond had formed among young men in such similar circumstances, and the evidence suggests that the Hungarian and the English princes became good friends.

In 1043, the elder of the Hungarians, Andrew, married Anastasia, daughter of Prince Jaraslow and Princess Ingegerd and, around the same time, a suitable marriage was arranged for Edward. His bride was named Agatha; she was German, the daughter of Luidolf, Margrave of Westfriesland (1008-38) and granddaughter of Bruno, Count of Brunswick (990-c.1013), whose wife Gisela would later marry Conrad II, emperor of Germany and Holy Roman Emperor. Bruno was the grandson of Conrad III, king of Burgundy, and cousin of another Gisela, who married King Stephen of Hungary. Indeed, Agatha's dazzling family connections have led to the notion that she must have been intended for Edmund, the elder prince, and only married Edward after his death. But although Edmund was certainly dead before he was forty, there is no evidence that Agatha was ever betrothed or married to him.

It is not known where the newlyweds spent the first couple of years of their life together, whether they stayed in the vast, timber-built palace at Kiev, or on Princess Ingegerd's estate on Lake Lagoda. Perhaps they paid visits to Agatha's family in Brunswick and Westfriesland, distance and slow transport being no hindrance to travel in the early Middle Ages. What seems certain is that princes Edmund and Edward spent time discussing their future with Prince Andrew; the situation in Hungary was coming to the boil and, when the action started, Andrew intended to be there.

King Stephen I died in 1038. After his falling out with Vászoly, he had adopted as his heir Peter Orseolo, the son of his half-sister who had married the Doge of Venice. Peter proved a poor substitute for the steely Stephen; his rule was challenged by disgruntled noblemen who, in 1041, deposed him in favour of Samuel Aba, another half-nephew of the late king. Samuel Aba, described by the Hungarian clergy as a savage who was unfit to rule, was in turn deposed, and in 1044 Peter Orseolo clawed back the throne. As the country slid into anarchy and renewed paganism, however, a group of rebellious Hungarian lords remembered the heir of Vászoly. Hurrying to Kiev, they assured Andrew of their support if he would return to Hungary and fight for the throne. Perhaps Andrew promised Edmund and Edward rich rewards in return for their aid, or perhaps, stateless and with no clearly defined future, they decided to throw in their lot with him anyway. It seems likely that when Andrew returned to Hungary, fought a quick, decisive campaign against the resurgent pagans and became king in 1046, the English princes went with him. Which brings us to the interesting question of when and where Edward's eldest child, Margaret, was born.

It is now generally believed that Margaret was born around 1046 – i.e. sometime between 1045 and 1047 – and it has been strongly suggested that a fortress in the mountains of southern Hungary was her birthplace. The site has been identified as Castle Reka, Mecseknadasd, a village twenty-five miles east of the regional capital Pécs. Much evidence has been found to back up the claim that members of the English royal house, who could only have been Edward and his family, did indeed live in the eleventh century at Mecseknadasd, close to an area once known as *terra britanorum*, the 'land of the Britons'. It thus seems that King Andrew I, as part of Edward's reward, granted him an estate in a part of the country that had been in the royal gift since King Stephen's time, and that Edward and Agatha brought up their children there. In pinpointing Margaret's birthplace, however, there is a complication.

It is known for certain that Andrew made his successful bid for the kingship of Hungary in 1046, following eight years of anarchy and misrule. It seems unlikely, however, that he was immediately in a position to distribute estates and other rewards; there would be pockets of resistance and the need to evict enemies before installing his friends. It seems equally unlikely that Prince Edward, assuming that he did march under the colours of Prince Andrew, would bring his young and well-connected wife, pregnant with her first child, into such a volatile situation; relations between the German and Hungarian dynasties were not entirely harmonious. More probable, surely, is that he would have left Agatha behind, either in Kiev or in some other friendly place, and sent for her to join him when the victorious Andrew had imposed order on his unruly realm.

It has been established that Margaret had no Hungarian blood. It is possible that she was not born in Hungary either. If she was born in 1045, she may well have been born in Kiev, or in the house of one of her mother's German relations. If it was 1046, and in Hungary, the birth must have followed immediately after Agatha's arrival and have been late in the year; it is hard to see how her parents could by then be resident on their new estate at Mecseknadasd. If she was born there in 1047, Edward and Agatha must have come very recently to live in the fortified wooden castle above the village. There is no known record of Margaret's birth, either there or anywhere else. It is not even known for certain that she was her parents' eldest child, though it is generally accepted that she was, and that she was followed by another girl, Christina. The third child was named after his English great great-grandfather, King Edgar – an interesting choice, proving that Prince Edward, however remote physically from England, was aware and proud of the dynasty to which he belonged. Edgar was said by the chronicler Orderic Vitalis to be the same age as William of Normandy's eldest son, Robert Curthose, who was born in 1053. He may have been a little older, though no more than fifteen at the time of the Norman Conquest in 1066.

3

A HUNGARIAN
CHILDHOOD

THE psychology of childhood is a post-Freudian preoccupation. Almost everyone nowadays accepts the impact of early experience on the growth and adjustment of the human psyche. It is agreed that, even when there is no conscious recall, a young child's feelings of real and imagined fear leave indelible marks, while love and security in infancy are the foundation of a happy, well-adjusted adult personality. It is also widely believed that the religious teaching of early years strongly affects the developing moral sense, and that it can either scar or enrich the mature imagination. These may be modern insights, but they cannot only be modern realities. Coping strategies have changed as the importance of early development has been better understood, but the experience itself must be the same. Margaret's adult personality was influenced by what happened to her when she was young, by the beliefs she absorbed, the fears she repressed and the stories she heard, as much as by her genetic inheritance. It is therefore worth considering the country in which she spent her first years, and the influences that may reasonably be assumed to have moulded her.

The Hungary of which Andrew I became ruler in 1046 was a land of mountain forests and grassy plains, the great Carpathian basin through which the rivers Tisza and Drava flowed to join the Danube, one of the great arteries of Europe. The Roman conquest of the areas known as Transdanubia and Transylvania had brought a brief period of classical influence on architecture and culture, but the withdrawal of the legions in the fifth century left a vacuum which Germanic tribes were eager to fill. Incursions of Visigoths, Huns, Ostrogoths, Lombards and Avars followed until, around 670, an invading force of Bulgaro-Turks took possession of the country. These settlers, whose linguistic legacy suggests Finnish as well as Turkish origins, are reckoned to have been the first Magyars. They were nomads, constantly seeking fresh pasturage for their flocks and herds of cattle and horses. They were also fearless fighters who sometimes hired themselves as mercenaries to neighbouring states, but more often went on the rampage for loot and slaves, terrorising communities from Bavaria to the Pyrenees. The Magyars were tribal in organisation and pagan in practice, worshippers of the old gods, with animistic beliefs and sorcerers as their spiritual leaders. Not until the tenth century did they decide to elect a single chief to co-ordinate attack and defence, choosing the heroic Árpád (c.870-907), whose dynasty, encompassing the reigns of Stephen I and Andrew I, endured until 1301.

The first significant figure in the progress of the Magyars towards Christian nationhood was Taksony, Árpád's grandson. By the middle of the tenth century, brutal Magyar raids on the Byzantine empire, Germany and Italy had finally drawn a unified response; a combined force of Germans and Czechs, under the leadership of the German emperor Otto I, crushed the Magyars at Lechfeld (modern Augsburg) in 955. In the wake of this humiliation, Taksony realised that the wellbeing of his nation – and its expansion westward – required peace with his neighbours and rapport with the new spirit of the age, Christianity. For these purely political reasons, he asked Pope John XII to send a bishop to his country – a suggestion that appealed more to the pope than to the German king who, determined not to have a papally-sponsored Magyar state on his doorstep, vetoed it.

It was not until the reign of Prince Géza, in the last years of the century, that Bishop Bruno, with the permission of Emperor Otto II, arrived at the head of a mission to Hungary. That he brought with him a group of military advisers is unsurprising in an era when the preaching of the Cross was routinely backed up by the unsheathing of swords. Géza, at the urging of his formidable Polish, Christian and Rome-friendly wife Adelhaid, was baptised and 'encouraged' his countrymen to follow his example, but although he married his daughters to Christian princes, his personal attitude to his new faith was ambivalent. Famously he boasted that, with wealth like his, he could afford to pay for sacrifices to both pagan and Christian gods – a hedging of bets which seems amusing now, but which was echoed in transitional societies all over Europe at that time.

There had been disagreement and schism within the Christian church since a bitter ninth-century quarrel between Pope Nicholas I and Photius, the patriarch of Constantinople (ancient Byzantium). It was caused, it has been said, by 'doctrinal misunderstanding, political blunder and personal ambition on both sides'. By the time of Géza, western Roman and eastern 'Orthodox' missionaries were competing for converts and Hungary's neighbours, Russia, Serbia, Bulgaria and the Byzantine empire, had already accepted the

Greek-based rites and beliefs of Orthodoxy. The zeal of Princess Adelhaid, who reputedly drank like a fish, rode like a cavalryman and had a truly awesome temper, may have been one reason why Orthodox missionaries made so little impression on Hungary; there were strong-minded royal wives long before Margaret married Malcolm III of Scots. Certainly by the time Adelhaid's stepson Stephen (István) succeeded his father as ruling prince in 997, Hungary was destined for the Roman sphere of influence.

Stephen, who had changed his name from Vajk at the time of his baptism, was a convinced Christian in a way that his father never was. Although he entered into a confederation of semi-autonomous states headed by Otto III, under the umbrella of the Holy Roman Empire, he believed that the best way to ensure a strong, truly independent Hungary was to link his fortunes directly with Rome. Encouraged by his mentor Bishop Adalbert of Prague (who would later be murdered by Prussian pagans irritated by his bossiness, and swiftly canonised in 999), he made determined efforts to impose western Christianity on his subjects. In 1000 he was rewarded by Pope Sylvester II with permission to call himself king; according to tradition, he was crowned at his birthplace, Esztergom, on Christmas Day 1000 and, early the following year, received from the pope not only the the title Apostolic King of Hungary but also a precious gift. Part at least of the 'Crown of Hungary', one of that country's most beautiful and emotive relics, was in the possession of King Stephen more than a thousand years ago.

It is difficult for modern people, whose model of sainthood is Mother Teresa of Calcutta, to see just what was saintly about a man like Stephen. He was a ruthless political operator, who had consolidated his rule by ousting rival chieftains and confiscating their lands. He was indifferent to bloodshed in his pursuit of a self-sufficient, unified Hungary, and his blinding and deafening of Vászoly – not the only member of his own family to experience the violence of his displeasure – horrifies us because, although we have seen acts of cruelty just as appalling in our own day, we tend not to confer sanctity on their perpetrators. It has been pointed out, however, that it is futile to judge the medieval mentality on the analogy of modern sensitivities; instead we must at least try to understand the mindset of men who had been reared in violent times, and who believed themselves charged by God with imposing social and religious change on recalcitrant populations.

The Catholic historian and sociologist Christopher Dawson (1889-1970) spoke of two parallel societies in early medieval Europe, the peace-society of the church and the war-society of the feudal nobility. The war-society might be affected superficially by the influence of the peace-society, but its real concerns were of a more aggressive, political kind. Stephen was probably better than most warlords; his devotion to the church was sincere. He built a cathedral at Esztergom, welcomed Benedictine monks to his country, donated land to support monasteries and ordered every tenth village to build a church and pay for a priest. He struck coins for the first time, gave Hungary a code of laws, encouraged the invention of a Latin alphabet for the Magyar tongue and made Latin the language of court and diplomacy. But he forbade marriage between Christians and pagans, and punished brutally breaches of the law. It was in recognition of a zeal untroubled by the paradox of imposing a religion of peace with the sword that he was canonised in 1093.

Just as Stephen's militant piety was a far cry from the vacillation of his father Géza, King Andrew I showed none of the compromise with paganism that had got his father Vászoly into such trouble. Although he could have had no affection for the king who had blinded Vászoly and exiled his sons, Andrew was the spiritual heir of Stephen. He had had to fight for his throne and was tenacious of power, but his court at Esztergom, forty-five miles up the Danube from modern Budapest, was a centre of Roman Catholic piety and it is fairly assumed that there Margaret had her first glimpse of Christian court life. She must have attended Mass in the church built by King Stephen and dedicated to St Adalbert, at a time when churches all over Europe were being adorned and enriched by kingly gifts, and observed the gulf between the magnificence of the court and the squalor of the city streets. Her later fluency in Latin suggests that her education began early, and it is possible that her teachers were, as later in England, Benedictine nuns. It is impossible to know how much time Margaret actually spent at court, but it is reasonable to suppose that, since the king was mainly resident in Esztergom in the winter and had granted Prince Edward an estate a hundred miles further south, she and her sister and brother would at least have spent their childhood summers among the wooded hills at Mecseknadasd.

It has been assumed, during the years of believing that the sons of Edmund Ironside were reared at the court of King Stephen, that Margaret's intense Catholic piety was an inheritance from her father, as well as her supposedly Hungarian mother. It has been suggested that when, thirty years later, she was troubled by the discrepancies between the practices of the Roman and the Scottish 'Celtic' churches, part of her 'problem' was that she knew nothing of any church but the one in which she was brought up. Without doubt Agatha, as a member of the German royal house, was within the Roman

Catholic fold, but if, as this narrative suggests, her father actually spent his formative years at the court of Prince Jaraslow at Kiev, Margaret's background was really more complicated. Kiev, a cosmopolitan town with Jews and Muslims among its population, had been officially Christian since 988, when its ruling prince Vladimir, married to a daughter of the Byzantine emperor, had adopted the beliefs and rituals of the eastern Orthodox church. Prince Jaraslow was an energetic Christian who, during Prince Edward's childhood, had built a cathedral famous for its thirteen cupolas and dedicated to the great symbol of Orthodoxy, Saint Sophia, the Holy Wisdom. Since the quarrel of Pope Nicholas I and Patriarch Photius in 858, Orthodox and Roman relations had worsened, and throughout the decades leading to the final schism in 1054 the two branches of Christendom were at loggerheads. It seems likely that, when he married Agatha and threw in his lot with Prince Andrew, it seemed expedient to Prince Edward simply to step from one tradition into the other – and perhaps, in the prevailing atmosphere of hostility, to keep quiet about the church from which he had transferred.

No one can know how much time Margaret spent in the company of her parents. Certainly the chief adult companions of royal children have always been nurses, tutors and servants, although it is possible that, as strangers in a foreign land, the English Æthelings, the 'princely family', were more intimate than most. Whether they were or not, however, it is hard to believe that Margaret grew up ignorant of her father's past, which was so pertinent to her own identity. She must have heard of her grandfather's heroic battle with Cnut and of his sudden, inadequately explained death, of her father's miraculous escape from England as an infant, his long journey across Europe as a twelve-year-old and his soujourn at the cosmopolitan court of Prince Jaraslow. But that she knew nothing of Orthodox Christianity is obvious from her later dogmatism, and it is tempting to think that an opportunity to broaden her mind was lost. As queen in Scotland she proved famously intolerant of any point of view but her own and, in her drive to bring the Scottish church into line with Rome, seems to have been oblivious to far more catastrophic division elsewhere.

It was not, however, Margaret's lot to live in a broad-minded age. If her views now seem blinkered, they arose from her intense, obedient western Catholic upbringing. Living in a country recently and forcibly converted, where paganism was still being practised underground and Christian stability by no means secure, a horror of heresy was bred in Margaret from infancy. She was taught that heterodox beliefs were abhorrent to God, that the Roman church was The Church, its doctrines right, its message absolute, its teaching the only guide to a good and holy life. Whatever her natural childish experiences, bad dreams, loneliness in the dark, fear of demons and danger lurking in the forest, she learned to counter them by absolute trust in an all-knowing, all-seeing God – a faith learned in childhood that would be the lodestar of her whole life. For as well as political conversion, where peoples were forced into Christianity by their rulers, there also existed a conversion of conviction, in which individuals found faith as an intense, self-defining experience. It was personal Christianity, with its hope of salvation and life everlasting, that provided meaning in a world of brutality, disaster, bereavement and early death.

At the same time, both by teaching and through observation, Margaret learned the hierarchical view of mankind that prevailed in Europe throughout the medieval period. On the top rung of the social ladder were emperors, kings and popes. One rung down were the nobility, bishops and abbots, and below them the middle ranks of knights, squires and merchants. At the bottom of the ladder were peasants, slaves and the urban poor, for ever stuck in the place God had ordained for them. This social system was approved by the church, which pointed to the similar chain of being in heaven, where God reigned supreme over archangels and angels, seraphim and cherubim – a tidy authorising of the mundane order by reference to the celestial. A religious virtue was made out of knowing one's place and, for all that a woman's status depended on her father's or her husband's, we can be sure that from her earliest years Margaret knew hers.

King Cnut died in 1035. His wife, Emma of Normandy, had previously been married to Margaret's great-grandfather, Æthelred 'the Unready', with whom she had two sons, Alfred, who was murdered in 1036, and Edward (canonised in 1161 and known to history as 'the Confessor'). During the years when their mother was married to Cnut, these young men lived in exile in Normandy. With Cnut, Emma had another son, Harthacnut, who on his father's death suceeded him as king of Denmark. The kingship of England, after two years of dithering and conditional regency, was given to Harold Harefoot, the son of Cnut and an ealdorman's daughter, Ælgifu of Northampton, to whom he may have been bigamously married. Never much more than a cipher – his mother being the power behind the throne – Harold died in 1040, just as Harthacnut was preparing to invade England and depose him. The death of Harthacnut two years later brought to an end the male line of Cnut, separated England from Denmark and cleared the way for Edward, son of Æthelred, to become king. He was the half-brother of Edmund Ironside, and uncle of Edward, Margaret's father, who had spent twenty-six years in exile. He was to remain in exile for sixteen years more.

King Edward, who would reign until 1066, was married to Edith, the eldest child of Earl Godwin of Wessex, the most powerful and pushy nobleman in England. The marriage was childless and the succession problematic; although the king had the right to name a successor and blood kinship with the king counted in the claimant's favour, it was not in itself enough. Even the closest kinsman could be rejected by the *witan*, the council of 'wise men' consisting mainly of nobles, bishops, abbots and ealdormen, if he were deemed too young, too weak or otherwise unsuitable. King Edward himself seems to have enjoyed teasing pretenders, notably his distant cousin Duke William of Normandy and Queen Edith's brother Harold Godwinsson, with hints, if not outright promises of support. He also decided in 1054, after consultation with the *witan*, to recall from exile the man who had the strongest blood claim to be the next king of England, his nephew Edward Ætheling.

As is pointed out by Alan J. Wilson in his book *St Margaret Queen of Scotland*, the most interesting thing about this summons is that, to all appearances, Edward and his brother Edmund had been expunged from English record in 1016. Cnut had made no attempt to track them down, no evidence exists that anyone in England had kept in touch with the princes, and they might reasonably have been thought to be dead. Now, suddenly, it seemed to be common knowledge that Edward Ætheling was in Hungary, that he was married with children, and that his elder brother had predeceased him. It must be assumed that discreet tracking of the princes had been undertaken during the years of Danish rule by those privately loyal to the old Saxon house, and it seems likely that the chief of these was Ealdred, the bishop of Worcester, who would become a leading light in the resistance to the Norman invasion in 1066. Trouble had been rumbling in England; years of friction between King Edward and the presumptuous Earl Godwin had come to a head with the entire Godwin family's expulsion from England in 1051 and their triumphant – and to the king humiliating – restoration only a year later. There was also a perception, perhaps exaggerated, of increased Norman officiousness and meddling in English affairs, and of Duke William of Normandy getting too big for his boots. It may have seemed a good time to point out to the Godwins and to the Normans that the king had a close relation with an indisputable claim to the throne.

In 1054, Bishop Ealdred and Abbot Ælfwine of Romsey were despatched to the court of Henry III, Emperor of Germany at Cologne. They were instructed to ask the emperor, on behalf of King Edward and the *witan*, to send ambassadors to King Andrew I of Hungary, requesting permission for Edward Ætheling and his family to return, via Germany, to England. Since King Edward's half-sister Gunnhild had been the emperor's first wife, his co-operation may have been taken for granted, but although Ealdred and Ælfwine were received with great courtesy, entertained for a year and loaded with gifts, their request was either ignored or turned down. It has been suggested that frosty relations between Germany and Hungary made the emperor unwilling to allow Andrew I's ally to travel through his territory. It was 1056 before the death of Henry III and the accession of the six year-old Henry IV, under the regency of his mother Agnes of Poitou, brought a change of heart. Permission was finally granted for the journey that would change the life of Margaret and her siblings for ever.

How Prince Edward felt about leaving Hungary to travel with his wife and three children, the youngest under five, to a remote kingdom with such distressing family associations, is nowhere recorded. Presumably he could have turned down his uncle's invitation, and continued to live in Hungary as an honoured guest and beneficiary of the king's largesse. Perhaps he was happy in this role, and accepted the summons reluctantly, from a sense of duty. It is also possible that he had always carried a burden of bitterness about the usurpation of his and his brother's rights, resented his position as a dependent at the courts of other princes and coveted his place in the sun. It is not known either how Princess Agatha liked the prospect of a second resettlement among foreigners whose language she did not know, or whether she wanted to be a queen – not that her preferences would have counted for much anyway. As soon as leave for the journey had been obtained, the forty year-old Edward Ætheling packed his worldly goods and treasures and, with his family and a party of retainers and servants, left Hungary for the land of his birth.

4

ENGLISH
INFLUENCES

L ONG before it became fashionable for hordes of pilgrims to cross the
English Channel *en route* to shrines as distant as Rome, that of St James
of Compostela in northern Spain, and the holy sepulchre at Jerusalem, travel
throughout Europe was as common as it was – by our standards – uncomfortable. The straight, durable roads built by the Romans to transport their
armies were, in the aftermath of empire, appropriated for less martial travellers,
and the long rivers of the continent provided relatively swift and easy movement from landlocked countries to the sea coast. It is hard not to imagine
Prince Edward, Princess Agatha and their young family, saddle-sore or bruised
from miles of bumping in unsprung carts through the rough terrain of central
Europe, but their long journey, though stressful, would have been more
comfortable than most. Edward was entitled to princely respect, his loyalty
to King Andrew had made him rich and the retinue of servants ensured that
the family travelled in style. And since they now passed through the emperor's
territory with permission, they would be hospitably entertained in palaces and
monasteries along the way.

It is not known what route the royal party took, but three possibilities
present themselves. By any of these the first stage of the journey would have
taken them by ship on the Danube from Esztergom to Pressburg (Bratislava),
then by a land route through Moravia to the Bohemian capital Prague,
dominated by the circular church built by Duke Wenceslas a century before.
From Prague the party from Hungary may have gone north to join the River
Elbe, which flows into the North Sea at the port now called Cuxhaven.
Alternatively they may have gone overland through the Thuringian forest to
Mainz and down the Rhine to Rotterdam, or overland via Cologne to the
port of Quentovic (Dieppe) at the mouth of the River Canche. Much of
Anglo-Saxon trade with the continent passed through Quentovic, and from
there was the most frequented Channel crossing to England.

Whichever way was chosen, the distances covered were immense and the journey must have taken many weeks. Before she reached the island where she would spend the rest of her life, Margaret passed through some of the wildest, most awe-inspiring tracts of a continent where towns were small, bandits roamed and the countryside was ravaged by one conflict after another. Since the family is known to have arrived in England in the early spring of 1057, part at least of the journey must have taken place in winter – although since their lives were contained within the 'Little Optimum', a period between 950 and 1300 when the weather was markedly milder, they may have been spared the severe frosts and wind chill of more recent central European winters. But however well-cushioned the carriages and sumptuous the family's accommodation in the stern of the royal longship, the children must often have been cold and weary and wondering if their wandering would ever end.

When the family finally came ashore in England, probably in London, Prince Edward was no doubt greeted ceremoniously, but his uncle was not there to meet him. Nor was he invited to court in the brief period of life that remained to him. The *Anglo-Saxon Chronicle* states what happened bleakly:

> *This year came Edward Ætheling, son of King Edmund, to this land, and soon after died ... we know not for what reason it was done, that he should not see his relation, King Edward.*

It is not known either of what Edward Ætheling died; the convenience of his demise makes it possible that another claimant, seeing him as a threat to long-held ambition, had him murdered, but it seems more likely that he died of natural causes. He was buried in St Paul's Minster in London beside his grandfather King Æthelred, leaving a family whose grief could scarcely have exceeded their bewilderment.

In *The Normans in Scotland* (1954) R. L. G. Ritchie pointed out that the notion of Agatha and her brood as poor relations dependent on the charity of the English king was unsupported by writers closer to them in time. Ailred of Rievaulx (c.1110-96), the Cistercian monk who had been a page at the court of Margaret's youngest son King David I and companion of her grandsons, wrote of the gold and artistic treasures bestowed upon Edward Ætheling by Andrew I of Hungary, while Turgot claimed that Margaret brought to Scotland great riches given to her father by King Edward and the German emperor. One of the treasures from Hungary, according to Ailred, was the Black Rood of Scotland, the ebony-carved crucifix contained in a gold casket and reputedly containing a fragment of the true Cross. (This sacred relic, said by Ailred to have inspired the building by King David of Holyrood Abbey in Edinburgh, was removed from Scotland by Edward I of England in 1291. Although returned briefly to the Scots in the fourteenth century, it again fell into English hands and was placed in St Cuthbert's shrine at Durham. During the rioting that followed Henry VIII's suppression of the cathedral in 1540, it disappeared.)

However well endowed materially, however, Agatha and her children were in need of protection and, whatever his reason for not receiving his nephew, King Edward now behaved well. Agatha was suitably housed and allowed to keep the Hungarian servants who wished to stay with her (several Scottish families claim, without much evidence, descent from these Hungarians). The tiny Edgar was allowed the title 'Ætheling' – not an endorsement of his claim, only an admission that he was 'throne-worthy' like his father. But both he and his sisters were clearly welcomed by the childless royal couple; according to *Vita Ædwardis Regis*, the 'Life of King Edward' later commissioned by Queen Edith, she herself 'zealously reared, educated, adorned and showered with motherly love those children who were said to be of royal stock'. If true, one wonders how Agatha felt about this hijacking of her maternal role; it has often been asked why, considering her language difficulty and the eclipse of her expectations, she did not cut her losses, take her children and go back where she belonged. This is to suggest that she had more power than she had; the hard fact was that if the king wanted the children to stay in England and she was unwilling to leave them, Agatha had no choice. Given her beliefs, she no doubt saw in her misfortune the chastisement of God to which she was bound to submit; on a more worldly level she must have consoled herself with the hope that her fortunes might yet be transformed. If Edgar found favour in court and country, she would one day be the mother of the king of England.

King Edward's was an ambiguous character. He was tall, good-looking and given to spectacular outbursts of temper. History has equated his piousness with a somewhat anaemic character; he has been presented as lacking energy and fonder of hunting than of statesmanship. Modern scholarship, however, suggests a different view. Edward was active against the Vikings during his father's reign, fought valiantly alongside his half-brother Edmund Ironside at Assandûn, and in the early part of his reign proved a vigorous and resourceful king. Exiled in his mother's home country, Normandy, during the reigns of Cnut and his sons, he has been accused of bringing to the English court an undue fondness for Norman manners and fashion, and of offending many of his Saxon courtiers by his promotion of Norman clergy and knights. It now seems that such patronage was slighter than supposed, and that the spread of Norman style and culture was simply an unstoppable trend.

Even so, Edward was himself half-Norman, and the fear of foreigners taking over was visceral. The early years of the reign were turbulent; Edward's election was not entirely popular and he was obliged to Earl Godwin for support – a debt he payed handsomely by marrying the earl's daughter. Although Edward proved himself capable of dealing quite ruthlessly with upstarts – including his mother, whom he never forgave her preference for his half-brother Harthacnut – the descent into acrimony of his personal relationship with Godwin and the struggle to placate warring factions among the nobility may have enervated him. After Godwin's death in 1052, he passed much of the burden of government to the earl's sons, Harold, Tostig, Gyrth and Leofwine, with whom he got on well. By the time the Æthelings arrived in England, he was devoting much time to the church, notably to the building of a great abbey at Westminster, dedicated to St Peter. From 1057 until 1066, young Edgar was a member of the royal household, moving between the king's residences at London, Winchester, Gloucester and Oxford. He received formal education in religion, languages and martial arts and, as the crisis of succession drew ever closer, informal education in power politics and intrigue. The education considered suitable for his sisters was of a different kind.

It has been said, in the absence of precise information, that Margaret and Christina were educated at court by Benedictines appointed to tutor them, but there seems no reason for such an arrangement. The young princesses were not so exalted as to merit special treatment, and there were several convent schools, within a twenty-mile radius of the king's seat at Winchester, that catered for an exclusively aristocratic clientele. Thirty years later, Margaret would send her own young daughters to be educated at Romsey Abbey, where her sister Christina became a nun in 1085, and the balance of probability is that she herself spent several years in a similar establishment, visiting court at the great holidays of Easter, Pentecost and Christmas, or when otherwise commanded by the king. The aristocratic, fashionable convent at Wilton Abbey near Salisbury is the most likely choice; Queen Edith herself had been educated there and had withdrawn within its walls during the awkward period when her father and brothers had been exiled by her husband. By 1057 Wilton was her special project; she was paying for the rebuilding in stone of the abbey church and endowing it with relics shamelessly filched from other shrines. Her old school would have seemed a perfect place for the princesses in whom she took such a motherly interest.

Many Anglo-Saxon nunneries were small, humble communities, but those like Wilton and Romsey were famous not only for their social cachet but also for the culture and scholarship of the nuns. The pattern of the Benedictine nunnery was standard; a fenced enclosure contained church, chapter house, refectory, kitchen, dormitories, schoolrooms, library and *scriptorium* and, at a small distance from the other buildings, an infirmary and the discreetly named *necessarium*. Generally the buildings were of wood and wattle with roofs thatched with reeds or straw, although in the better-endowed foundations wooden churches were being replaced with stone. Although the Rule of St Benedict demanded poverty, the aristocratic houses had become communally wealthy through royal patronage, dowries, rents and donations to the shrines they operated. Wilton owned mills, houses and pasture rights; it received rents paid in wool and donations for building and decoration. Romsey owned land in Wiltshire and Hampshire, and its income was the envy of many male monasteries.

At Wilton, the average number of inmates in Margaret's time was fifty; all were under the authority of a prioress, but only the core were consecrated virgins vowed to the monastic ideal of poverty, chastity and obedience. The rest were lay sisters who did the cooking, laundry, gardening and manual work, older women who had decided to devote their widowhood to contemplation, and schoolgirls under the supervision of a nun called the Mistress of the Maidens. These young women were expected to follow a diluted version of the Benedictine Rule and to dress soberly, as were the nuns; the strictly uniform habit belonged to a later age. A few had a religious vocation and would stay in the cloister; most, like upper-class girls down the ages, had been sent to boarding school to be trained in good manners and accomplishments, and given enough academic education to make them companionable to their husbands when the time came to marry. In many nunneries they were allowed to wear jewellery and keep pets, and dancing was not forbidden. Although she must have shared their lessons in Latin, French, music and needlework, dined with them and picked up enough English to understand their chatter at the recreation hour, it is impossible to imagine Margaret finding much in common with such a group. She was like Leoba, the ninth-century nun of whose convent girlhood it was said that *she found no pleasure in aimless jests and wasted no time on girlish romances, but, fired with the love of God, fixed her mind always on reading or hearing the word of God.*

After the trauma and upheaval of 1056-57, the opportunity to study and pray in a safe, orderly environment must have been a colossal relief, and it is small wonder that Margaret and her sister found the cloister so appealing.

From Turgot's *Life*, and from other sources, we know at least some of the books which Margaret read during her adolescent years, proof that able pupils were stretched academically and that in Anglo-Saxon England women were considered as capable intellectually as men. Besides the psalms and Gospels and the legends of saints, she gained some acquaintance with the theological works of the early 'Christian Fathers', the *Morals and Homilies* of St Gregory (540-604), the *Collations* of Cassian (360-430), which were read aloud in Benedictine houses before Compline, the last service of the day, and the *Confessions* and *The City of God* of St Augustine (354-430). She also studied the Rule of St Benedict, which affected her profoundly for the rest of her life.

Benedict, who was born at Nursia in Umbria around 480, was the father of western monasticism. He is said to have studied in Rome but, appalled by the dissolute behaviour of the citizens as the empire collapsed, withdrew to a cave in the mountains at Subiaco, forty miles from the city. In a great wave of enthusiasm for the monastic way of life, so many men came to join him that he was able to set up twelve communities, with twelve monks in each. In 529 he left Subiaco to found the great monastery at Monte Cassino, half way between Naples and Rome, and there wrote his Rule, based on the famous exhortation *ora et labora*, 'pray and work'. The whole monastic day was filled with these complementary activities, with only two brief breaks, one for dinner and short recreation, the other for a three-hour sleep.

Benedict laid down regulations for everything; how services were to be conducted, how the sick, young and aged were to be treated, how charity should be dispensed, how the monk or nun should behave in every situation. All must do manual work, regardless of their status in the outside world; chastity, humility, service and obedience were the great virtues, silence was golden and laughing out loud was forbidden. To the modern mind such a life may seem exhaustingly austere, but for many centuries it was regarded as a model of spiritual rigour and physical moderation. This was largely because the thrust of Benedict's message was, in its time, revolutionary: 'If you really are a servant of Jesus Christ, let the chain of love hold you firm, not a chain of iron.'

Although Benedict was not against physical chastisement, the Rule came down hard on fanaticism. Practices like excessive fasting, self-torture and brutal punishment were outlawed; each individual was to have enough for his needs, but no more.

By the time when Margaret was receiving her education and apparently thinking of a life in religion, the original, socially inclusive Rule of St Benedict had been modified considerably. It had become clear over the years that there were not enough hours in the day for all the prayer and work Benedict thought necessary and, in the tenth century, a drastic reform initiated at the French monastery at Cluny effectively separated the two functions. In future, manual labour in kitchen, garden and farm would be done by lay brothers and sisters, leaving the consecrated religious free to concentrate on the *opus dei*, the 'work of God' centred on praise and intercessory prayer. Benedict's gospel-informed idea of holy equality was the casualty of this move; inevitably the lay personnel of the community were of lower social status, and aristocratic nunneries like Wilton could not have existed had they not mirrored the secular society of their time. In the more egalitarian society of the twenty-first century the paradox seems glaring, but it is unlikely to have troubled Margaret. Her orthodoxy was that of the church in her own hierarchical time, and she would have accepted unquestioningly that a system designed for a more compact, less sophisticated Christian society would no longer work. It was the personal demands of the Benedictine Rule, with its uncompromising insistence on the Christian virtues of obedience, humility, self-denial, charity and the service of God that fired her serious, ardent adolescent soul. But however much she yearned for the order and security of the cloister, she was not immune to other influences which, in the long term, would have just as great an influence on the conduct of her adult life.

Margaret's lifetime coincided with the beginning of the medieval age when kings and queens, uneasily aware of the tension between their own wealth and the ideal of holy poverty, began to seek favour in the afterlife by enriching God's church on earth. The mania for endowing and beautifying abbeys and churches had many spectacular results, and incidentally provided years of work for masons, carpenters, sculptors, goldsmiths and embroiderers. Englishwomen, particularly nuns, were so skilled in ecclesiastical gold-thread embroidery that the style was called *opus anglicanum*, 'English work'. Margaret certainly learned this holy art, and saw inspiring examples in the vestments, curtains and altar cloths made for the Old and New Minsters at Winchester.

She handled, and probably owned books illustrated in the richly illuminated style now known as the 'Winchester School'. On her visits with the peripatetic court to London, she must have seen the great abbey church at Westminster under construction (it was completed just in time for King Edward's burial before the high altar in January 1066). At Wilton, if she was indeed educated there, she must also have witnessed the rebuilding of the church under the patronage of Queen Edith, and it is likely that these acts of largesse, coupled with royal almsgiving, formed her adolescent view of the good use to which the wealth of Christian monarchs might be put.

The court had another important lesson to teach. King Edward had begun his reign far from being the Frenchified dandy of legend; he had spent his early years as a fighting man and, during his exile in Normandy, had lived as a simple knight, devoted to hunting and indifferent to courtly fashion. This casual state of affairs continued through his bachelor years as king, but was set to change dramatically when in 1045, aged about forty, he married Edith, eldest daughter of Earl Godwin and his Danish wife Gytha. Edith was in her early twenties, reputedly beautiful, intelligent, religious and chaste, but also determined and imperious, as attested by the monks from whose churches she demanded treasures to enrich her own. Her education at Wilton had introduced her to high culture; she had learned to read Latin and had acquired several languages, besides expertise in the *opus anglicanum* and other arts.

Not surprisingly, her husband's downbeat lifestyle did not appeal to Edith, who saw the trappings of majesty as an essential adjunct to authority. Before he had time to protest, the unpretentious middle-aged soldier found himself ablaze with glory, rigged out in embroidered robes, hung with gold and jewels, even carrying a walking-stick studded with gems. His saddle and bridle jingled with little animals and birds made of gold, a lofty new throne was designed, his spartan hall was curtained and its rush-strewn floor made bright with magnificent carpets from Spain. At the same time, Edith made herself indispensable to him, modest in public but an eager and, when it came to the promotion of her family's interests, sometimes forceful counsellor behind the scenes. It is impossible to know how intimate Edith and Margaret really were, but Margaret was intelligent and observant. Even if she did not then see her future in court life, in Edward's young wife she had an unforgettable example of queenly practice for reference in the years to come.

5

CONQUEST

W HEN King Edward died on 5 January 1066, Margaret was about twenty years old. At a time when the betrothal and even marriage of eligible princesses barely beyond infancy was commonplace, the fact that she was still single may indicate that her wish to be a nun had been taken seriously by her pious foster father. She was too old to be a schoolgirl, and where she spent her later teenage years is unknown. Even if she was in a nunnery, it is hard to suppose that she heard no rumour of the cataclysmic events unfolding outside the wall. If she was living anywhere near the court, she must have known as well as anyone that the peaceful world she had enjoyed for the past nine years was on the verge of disintegration.

King Edward's reign had ended in personal humiliation. Of Earl Godwin's four sons, the eldest, Harold, had effectively become the king's coadjutator, but both Edward and Edith had a soft spot for Tostig, who had been entrusted with the earldom of Northumbria. Tostig, unfortunately, was less loved by the Northumbrians, who resented the harshness of his rule. In 1065, while he was away visiting the king in Wiltshire, they staged a bloody revolt and demanded his replacement by Morcar, whose elder brother Edwin was sub-ruler of Mercia, the vast and once independent earldom which most probably took its name from its western frontier, the marches or borderland of Wales. Edward did his best to pour oil on troubled waters by holding a council at Britford near Salisbury, but reconciliation was not in the air. Simmering anger and jealousy between Harold and Tostig came to the boil; Tostig accused his brother publicly of pre-arranging his downfall and Harold, to the fury of both king and queen, took umbrage and refused to fight for Tostig's reinstatement. It is fair to say that Tostig had grounds for suspicion; Harold was closely allied to Edwin and Morcar, and a year later would marry their sister. The result of the quarrel was, however, disastrous. As the year's end approached, the king was obliged to give in to the rebels and Tostig, deprived of his earldom, was forced by the continuing violence of the insurgents to flee with his wife and child to her brother Count Baldwin's court in Flanders. Tostig as a loose cannon, snarling and hell-bent on revenge, was not good news.

Christmas that year should have been a joyful one. The court was in London for the dedication, on 28 December, of the king's new church at Westminster, said to be the most magnificent north of the Alps. It seems to have been then, in London, that King Edward finally named Harold as his chosen successor, a nomination endorsed by the *witan*. In doing so, he not only passed over the claim of his great-nephew Edgar, but also that of Duke William of Normandy, to whom he was less closely related but before whom he had also dangled the prospect of succession. He then seems to have had a stroke; too ill to attend the dedication of the church, he died on 4 January 1066. Harold wasted no time. Two days later, on the same day that King Edward was buried, he had himself crowned.

Edgar Ætheling undoubtedly had a hard deal. He did not have a strong enough party to back him, and it may be that during the years he had spent at court he had failed to impress the king. He was described by William of Malmesbury as 'silently sunk into contempt by his indolence', but that was much later, when failure and disappointment may well have soured him. More modern historians have dismissed him as ineffectual and lacking leadership skills, but what weighed most against him in 1066 was surely his youth. With the country under serious threat by enemies from abroad, an inexperienced teenager was bound to lose out against a battle-hardened warrior like Harold. Edgar was left to nurse his grievance, and no doubt his mother hers, while the future was driven by men much older and tougher and more ruthless than he.

The unseemly haste with which Harold had grabbed the crown caused raised eyebrows at home and moral outrage abroad. Rumours that he had broken an oath to help Duke William of Normandy to the throne would not go away; to renege on a solemn oath was, in the Middle Ages, among the most dastardly of crimes. No one was more outraged than Tostig, who added one more to his list of reasons for seeking revenge. The chronicler Orderic Vitalis claimed that Tostig approached Duke William with a proposal for a joint invasion, but met with a chilly reception; Duke William was well able to avenge himself. From Normandy Tostig apparently went to Norway, to the court of King Harald 'Hardrada', meaning 'the Ruthless'. Before 1045, Harald's nephew and predecessor had made a succession treaty with Harthacnut; this long-dead agreement was now ludicrously invoked to give legitimacy to Harald's eager acceptance of Tostig's suggestion that he should invade England and seize the throne.

It seems that Harald and Tostig agreed a partition of the country south of the Tees, while the north was held out as an enticement to Malcolm III, king of Scots, were he to join them. Malcolm and Tostig were old friends, and it was at Malcolm's court that Tostig spent the summer of 1066, having tried unsuccessfully, *en route* from Flanders, to invade Northumbria on his own behalf. By September the fearsome Viking Harald was ready to put to sea. He came via Orkney and Tostig, with supplies but no troops from the king of Scots, met up with him somewhere between the Firth of Forth and the estuary of the Tyne. Meanwhile across the English Channel at St-Valéry, at the mouth of the River Somme, the Norman fleet was also preparing to sail.

According to the *Life* of King Edward, on his deathbed he horrified his companions with a vision of a green tree, representing England. Within a year and a day of his death, he prophesied, God would punish the nation's sins by delivering it into the hands of its enemies, and devils would go through the land with fire, sword and the havoc of war. At Easter the appearance of a comet, beautifully described in the *Anglo-Saxon Chronicle* as 'a long-haired star', was seen as another portent of doom. All through the summer, Harold kept watch on the Channel coast, positioning a large force at strategic points from Kent to Dorset and stationing the fleet in the shelter of the Isle of Wight. By September, however, with the season of storms approaching, tension eased amid a general feeling that England was safe, at least until the spring. The coastal forces had already begun to drift home for the winter when news came of what was happening in the north.

Whatever his faults, Harold Godwinsson was a brave soldier. As soon as he heard that Harald Hardrada, Tostig and more than seven thousand Norsemen were approaching York, he called up the élite force of bodyguards and household troops known as housecarls and went north by the old Roman road. On 25 September, he fell upon a complacently unprepared Norse force at Stamford Bridge, thirteen kilometres from the city, and completely wiped it out. Of the three hundred longships that had brought the Norsemen to England, only twenty-four were needed to transport the survivors home. It must have been a good moment for Harold. He had seen off the Vikings, the terrifying Harald Hardrada was dead, and so was the principal thorn in his flesh, his brother Tostig. Sadly for him, his triumph was short-lived.

Only three days after Harold's stunning victory at Stamford Bridge, Duke William had left St-Valéry with a fighting force of ten thousand men, hundreds of horses and a castle in kit form – the *castellum* of the Bayeux tapestry. Two days later he landed at Pevensey, between Hastings and the modern town of Eastbourne. The castle was erected and while Harold, possessed by almost superhuman energy, rode south, the Normans – again according to the Bayeux tapestry – had time to go ravaging and looting in the country round about. When Harold stopped in London to muster fresh troops, he was, said Orderic Vitalis, so exhausted that his family was alarmed; his brother Gyrth offered to take his place as commander and, as he was leaving, his mother Gytha clung in terror to his knees. Such was his impatience that Harold kicked her aside. The two armies met at Senlac, near Hastings, on 14 October and, even after all the English had been through, the battle was finely balanced until late in the day. It was Harold's death – caused famously if controversially by an arrow through his eye – that knocked the stuffing out of his army. By nightfall his brothers Gyrth and Leofwine also lay dead on the battlefield, and with them the flower of the Anglo-Saxon nobility. It was one of the great turning points of European history.

Duke William met with little resistance as he cut his way through southern England, and by November he was at the gates of London. Instead of immediately hammering home his advantage, however, he decided to spend a few weeks brutally impressing his presence on the inhabitants of Surrey, Berkshire and the north of Hampshire. Meanwhile, in a last act of defiance, the surviving English earls rallied to the Anglo-Saxon claimant; in a meaningless ceremony in London Edgar Ætheling was elected, though not crowned king. The first Englishman to accept that the future was Norman was Archbishop Stigand of Canterbury, followed by Queen Edith, who acknowledged William's sovereignty (and retained her honourable position) at Winchester. In early December Edgar Ætheling, along with Archbishop Ealdred of York, who had negotiated his father's return from Hungary, earls Edwin of Mercia and Morcar of Northumbria, sundry nobility and representatives of the city of London, capitulated to William at Berkhampstead in Hertford-shire. The new king was crowned in Westminster Abbey on Christmas Day 1066, less than a year after the burial of King Edward and King Harold's coronation.

Where were Agatha and her daughters when these violent, life-changing events were taking place? Were they at Westminster when the new church was consecrated? Were they in Winchester when Queen Edith, ever pragmatic, submitted to the invader who had killed three of her brothers and snuffed out her dynastic dreams? Were they in London, tensely awaiting the

Conqueror's arrival, while their son and younger brother was vainly elected king of England? No one knows, because in the accounts of 1066 they were not considered worthy of mention. They had no status other than 'the mother and the sisters of the Ætheling', an adolescent boy who, by virtue of his sex and not his wisdom, was legally head of his family. They could do nothing without his consent, and his decisions would determine their lives for the foreseeable future.

It is one of history's mysteries why William I, in his time of triumph, did not arrange for Edgar Ætheling to be killed. A usurper is rarely tolerant of a minor whose claim may become a rallying-point for the loyal and disaffected, and William was not a soft-hearted man. Perhaps he felt some sympathy because he had himself had a troubled youth; certainly he dealt patiently with Edgar, awarding him the earldom of York and such honour as could be given while keeping him on a short leash. When, in 1067, William felt his grip on England secure enough to pay an extended visit to Normandy, Edgar and his former supporters earls Morcar and Edwin were among the prominent Englishmen he took with him. While the assertion of the chronicler William of Poitiers that Edgar was treated as one of William's dearest companions may be taken with a pinch of salt, there is nothing to suggest that the king harboured malign feelings towards the boy. If Edgar had buried his grudge and accepted the new regime, he and his sister Margaret might have lived pleasant, obscure lives in England. But Edgar, immature and robbed, as he no doubt saw it, of his rights, did not have forgiveness in mind.

Although the Conqueror had established an iron grip on the south-eastern region of England, he overestimated the willingness of the notoriously belligerent northerners to come to heel. Their soujorn in Normandy had not reconciled earls Morcar and Edwin to their new overlord and other prominent northern lords – Waltheof, son of the famous Earl Siward of Northumbria; Merleswein, sheriff of Lincoln; Cospatric, recently appointed earl of Northumbria and kinsman of the Scottish king – were equally disenchanted. One of William's earliest acts had been to impose heavy taxes on his northern 'subjects' which, on top of personal grievances (such as the thwarting of Earl Edwin's plan to marry William's daughter) brought simmering discontent to boiling point. Confident of help from Malcolm, king of Scots, who had an agenda of his own in Northumbria, they decided that they were strong enough to take on the Normans. Perhaps Earl Edwin and Earl Morcar thought that the Ætheling still had some mileage as a figurehead, or perhaps it was Edgar who, getting wind of an opportunity, decided that his ambition would be best served by joining them. In the summer of 1068 he gave his minders at court the slip and fled north, taking his mother and sisters with him.

It would be wrong to impute to Agatha, Margaret and Christina any reluctance to accompany Edgar on his adventure. Subsequent events prove that the Æthelings were a close family and, although both Margaret and Christina had an inclination for the cloister, neither had taken conventual vows. They may have felt that their brother's claim to the kingship of England should, for the present, take precedence over their own desires, and it would have been natural for Edgar's mother still to harbour hope on his behalf. The three women were, however, being drawn into a situation of great volatility and danger, and the next eighteen months must have been the most nerve-racking and uncomfortable of their lives.

In the event, the rebellion of 1068 came to nothing. King William's response to news of it was to send north one of his formidable fighting forces and, accepting reality, Earl Morcar and Earl Edwin again submitted to him. Bought off by William through the mediation of the bishop of Durham, the Scottish king had withdrawn his offer of help; Orderic Vitalis ends an unintentionally hilarious passage about the tranquil, peace-loving, pious nature of the Scots by remarking that on this occasion Malcolm 'consulted his own interest and greatly pleased his people, in that he preferred peace to war'. With King William grimly advancing towards York, for the remaining rebels a strategic withdrawal seemed the best option. 'Merleswein and Cospatric and all the most noble of the Northumbrian nation,' according to the chronicler Florence of Worcester, 'avoiding the king's austerity and fearing that they like others should be sent to prison, went by ship to Scotland, taking with them Prince Edgar and his mother Agatha and his two sisters Margaret and Christina.' For the first time in more than ten years, the Ætheling's womenfolk were granted a passing mention on the page of history.

It is at this point, however, that the legend of Margaret begins to elbow out the scanty factual record. A number of chroniclers, including Ailred of Rievaulx and John of Fordun, stated that the Æthelings had decided to return to Hungary, but were blown off course and arrived in Scotland, as it were, by mistake. At this particular point in their lives, however, this seems improbable; Hungary must by then have been a distant memory to them all, and Edgar certainly had not given up hope of the crown. But the motif of storm proved powerful; all the romantic accounts of Margaret's arrival in Scotland cast her as a refugee, tossed up by a tempest on the shore of the Forth 'at a place since called St Margaret's Hope', within convenient riding distance of the royal palace at Dunfermline. In fact, it is not known where the party of Northumbrian lords and Anglo-Saxon royalty landed, although they did find their way to Dunfermline. 'And there,' as Florence continued, 'with the peace of Malcolm, King of Scots, they passed the winter.'

There is an intriguing possibility that Malcolm and Margaret had encountered each other before. During the reign of Macbeth between 1040 and 1057, Malcolm had spent some years in exile at the English court, where he had got to know King Edward well. Although he was back in Scotland by the time of the Æthelings' arrival, he paid a courtesy visit, accompanied by the ill-fated Earl Tostig, to King Edward in 1059. According to Orderic Vitalis, Malcolm later claimed that 'King Edward, when he gave me Margaret, his great-niece, in wedlock, gave me the county of Lothian'. (Lothian, the eastern part of the Lowlands between the Forth and the Cheviots, was at this time still nominally possessed by the English crown; the opposite situation existed to the west in Cumbria, where Scottish influence remained long after effective control had passed to the English.) If Orderic's account is correct, it may be that King Edward's failure to expedite the marriage of his conventually-inclined ward explains Malcolm's otherwise unprovoked attack on Northumbria in 1061. At the time, Malcolm must have been more interested in the territory than the bride; there could have been little personal attraction between an intense, pious fourteen year-old schoolgirl and a Celtic warrior sixteen years her senior. Whatever the truth, a year or so after his visit to the English court in 1059, Malcolm was married to someone else.

6

THE KING OF SCOTS

I T is unclear, since the early chroniclers contradict one another and modern historians differ, whether the Æthelings spent the winter of 1068-69 in Scotland before moving south again in the spring, or whether Margaret arrived in 1068 for the first and only time. If she stayed, the (unrecorded) date of her marriage may have been as early as 1069, but the alternative and perhaps more persuasive scenario is that when Edgar, accompanied by Merleswein and Cospatric, travelled south in the spring of 1069 to join a renewed revolt against the Normans, his mother and sisters went with him. There is no record of where they were accommodated, although Alan J. Wilson suggests that they may have been the guests of Ethelwin, bishop of Durham. Certainly Edgar was with the insurgents when they beseiged the castle at York and when King William, responding to the slaughter of his appointed earl Robert de Comines and his followers at Durham, moved with corresponding brutality to relieve it. It is possible that the Æthelings then returned to Scotland, but if so they were on the move again by September, when news came that King Swein of Denmark, also hankering after the English throne, had sent his two sons with a huge expedition of ships and armed men into the Humber. Edgar, Merleswein and Waltheof assembled a fleet of their own and joined forces with them. In what must have seemed to the teenage Edgar his finest hour, English rebels and the Danes made a successful assault on York.

King Swein himself was now in England. Briefly it seemed that Edgar and his friends were at least on the winning side, but then things went downhill rapidly. Unfortunately for the rebels, by the crucial month of October the Danes had failed to establish a safe area in which to spend the winter. An exasperated King William arrived, bought off the Danes in time-honoured fashion and proceeded to give the rebels the thrashing of their lives. Towns, villages and farms were torched; whole populations were massacred while others fled in terror to the hills. The only sign of forgiveness in William was the pardoning of Cospatric, who was allowed to buy back the earldom of

Northumbria – most probably to prevent him from ganging up with his cousin Malcolm, king of Scots who, in the spring of 1070, bypassed Northumbria and invaded Yorkshire.

Modern historians are divided about Malcolm's motive for this, the second incursion of his reign. Some consider it opportunistic, a mere taking advantage of chaos to grab booty and slaves. Another theory is that, since William had recently brought Yorkshire and its people to the brink of annihilation, Malcolm saw a chance to finish the job for him; by isolating Northumbria from the rest of England, he would make it an easier target for his own expansionist ambitions. The most recent analysis sees in Malcolm's intervention a decision to support King Swein, who was still in the offing, and the Ætheling. Certainly Malcolm's method never changed; at the head of an army mainly composed of the notoriously fierce men of Galloway, he now cut a swathe of terror and desolation from the Vale of Eden to Teesdale and was at Wearmouth, according to Symeon of Durham, engaged in burning churches and their captive congregations when he had some unexpected visitors.

And there, while he rode by the banks of the river, and, looking forth from an elevated spot upon his men's cruel deeds wrought upon the wretched English, feasted his mind and his eyes with the sight, it was announced to him that Edgar Ætheling and his sisters, fair maidens of royal birth, and many other rich men fleeing from their estates, had come to shore in ships at that harbour.

This can hardly have been the most opportune moment for a visit. Malcolm, however, composed himself and when the Æthelings had 'commended themselves to him … he spoke to them kindly, and granted them with his firmest peace to dwell in his realm so long as they would, with all their followers'.

Perhaps it was really at this point that the Æthelings were on board ship with the intention of returning to Hungary. It would not be surprising if the events of the past eighteen months had crushed Edgar's spirits, terrified his mother and bewildered his sisters. But fate or King Malcolm's persuasion decreed otherwise. The flotilla of longships continued northward up the coast, past Lindisfarne, Berwick and St Abb's Head, and so again into the Firth of Forth. Behind them came Malcolm, stained, if Symeon is to be believed, with the blood of women and children, and driving before him hundreds of English youths destined to be slaves in perpetual exile.

Among the perceptions of the past most wounding to modern Scottish sensibilities are that Malcolm III, king of Scots was an illiterate barbarian and that his kingdom was an uncouth backwater fortunate in the civilising influence of English Margaret. That the principal sources of this sour account were the chronicler Symeon and the hagiographer Turgot is unsurprising; both were monks of Durham, a Northumbrian city which for years lived in terror of Scottish depredation and, after their clash at Melrose in 1074, there was probably no love lost between Malcolm and Turgot. A less partial view of Margaret's impact on the country of her adoption needs some understanding of its previous history, and a more dispassionate view of its ruler.

If, in early medieval times, Scotland seemed isolated culturally from the rest of Europe, the reasons were both geographical and political. The mountainous and difficult terrain had discouraged incursion since Roman times, and Scotland's peninsular situation, with no close neighbour except the one to which it was physically attached, had had consequences both good and bad. On the positive side, isolation had provided an environment in which the distinctive art of the Picts and the Scots could flourish; long before Margaret's time these Celtic peoples had made sculpture, jewellery, glass and metalwork of haunting beauty, high quality and original design. The church, built on the Irish model introduced by Columba (521-97), was vigorous, its monks chronicling events and producing exquisite illuminated manuscripts, such as the famous Book of Kells. The Scots brought with them from their northern Irish homeland *filidh*, poets who had to be learned in history and literature as well as adept at composing verse; through them came a vigorous tradition of storytelling and the oral transmission of the law.

The downside of such a culture was that its very self-containment made it vulnerable to attack and, whatever the cultural claims now made for the Vikings, their influence on Scotland in the ninth and tenth century was far from benign. Their attacks on the monastery of Iona, leading to its abandonment and the closing of its *scriptorium*, meant a massive loss of Scottish written record, and during the ninth and tenth centuries there is a sense of an indigenous culture withering and not being replaced by anything of comparable value. Danish Viking domination in central and northern England drove a wide cultural wedge between Scotland and the Anglo-Saxon south and, although Norse Viking raiding in Scotland subsided some time before the Danes stopped invading England, Scottish links with western Europe were only slowly re-established. There was no large influx of goods from countries like France, Italy or Spain, nor the accompanying commerce in fashion and new ideas with which, by the middle of the eleventh century, southern

England was advantageously in touch. Nor was Scotland much exposed to the prevailing wind in church affairs; its disjunction from the Roman communion had begun as long ago as 664, when the Celtic rites of the church of Columba had been rejected by an ecclesiastical council known as the Synod of Whitby. By the time of Malcolm III's accession in 1058, the usages of the Scottish church had no counterpart except in Ireland.

Scotland did, however, have one great strength. Although the Norse Vikings had settled in large numbers in Caithness and the Northern and Western Isles, establishing their own rule, in the rest of the country they had neither unseated nor replaced Scottish kings. Since the Picts and Scots had united under King Kenneth MacAlpin in 843, the country known as Scotland had absorbed Angles with links to England and Britons with links to Cumbria and Wales, but had remained predominantly a Celtic land, with a tradition of loyalty to one king. In Malcolm III it acquired one who was warlike, ruthless, determined to hold on to what had been dearly acquired and keen to push his border southward. His years in England had given him a more intimate knowledge of his southern neighbour than had been available to his predecessors, though whether his foreign policy was much influenced by it is questionable.

Whether or not Malcolm had been affianced to Margaret on his visit to King Edward's court in 1059, by the time when, according to the *Anglo-Saxon Chronicle*, he 'began to yearn for Edgar's sister', he was a man of thirty-nine, survivor of violent regime change, usurpation, exile, battle and ultimately restoration. If it is true that he could not read and write, it was not because he was incapable, but because in his time scholarship was the preserve of monks, nuns and clerics. Malcolm, not known in his own time as 'Canmore' or 'Big-head' (a moniker attached in the *Annals of Ulster* to his great-grandson, Malcolm IV, who is reckoned to have had Paget's disease), lived in a period when martial arts were the mainstay of a princely education, but he is reputed to have spoken Gaelic, English and French, and to have had some knowledge of Latin. He was the elder son of Duncan I – not the wise, benign old man of Shakespeare's play but an inept ruler in early middle age – who in 1040 was murdered by his kinsman Macbeth. Malcolm and his younger brother Donald fled in different directions; for the next seventeen years Malcolm was under the protection of Edward, the English king. He also spent time at York, in the household of Earl Siward of Northumbria, who was probably his maternal uncle. When in 1054 Earl Siward, with the help of forces supplied by King Edward, invaded Scotland and engaged Macbeth, traditionally at Dunsinnan Hill in Perthshire, the purpose of the expedition was to restore

Malcolm as a trusted and reliable vassal of the English king. (Such vassalage was an established custom which did not seriously prejudice the independence of the Scottish ruler; in practice it was little more than an acknowledgement of the manifestly superior clout of the English state, and a promise to be its king's 'sworn helper', i.e. not to act in a way detrimental to English interests.) The hard-won victory at Dunsinnan Hill would give the young king control of Scotland south of the Tay, but it was 1057 before he slew Macbeth at Lumphanan in what is now Aberdeenshire, and 1058 before, by having Macbeth's stepson Lulach ambushed and killed at Essie in Strathbogie, he took possession of the whole kingdom.

If King Edward expected gratitude and compliance in Malcolm, however, he must have been disappointed. Up to a point, Malcolm was a southerner; Prince of Cumbria by hereditary right and its ruler since 1054, on his accession he had chosen Dunfermline as his principal seat rather than a more traditionally Celtic site such as Dunkeld or Abernethy. Yet for all his lack of what seemed to many of his subjects Celtic credentials, his long exposure to Anglo-Saxon and tangentially to Norman culture does not seem to have influenced him much. Nor, although he was a baptised Christian (his grandfather, Crinan, was lay abbot of Dunkeld), was he noticeably impressed by the conspicuous piety of the English court. Early in his reign he sought friendship with the Scandinavian rulers of the Northern Isles and, around 1060, married Ingibiorg Finnsdottir, who may have been the widow but was more probably the daughter of Thorfinn, Earl of Orkney. This was an intelligent alliance, which countered native suspicion of the English-educated king; Ingibiorg was related to both Norse and Celtic families and the marriage secured for Malcolm peace on his northern frontier. It produced at least two sons, Duncan and Donald; a man called Malcolm who witnessed a charter of King Duncan II at Durham in 1094 may have been a third.

In his attitude to his erstwhile benefactors, the young king was more ambivalent. The death of Earl Siward in 1055 had ended a long personal loyalty and, although his polite visit to the English court in 1059 may have been to renew the traditional oath of loyalty to the English king, Malcolm soon set the pattern of his subsequent oathtaking by breaking it. At that time, Northumbria still stretched from the Forth to the Humber, and for all that its northern section, Lothian, had effectively been under Scottish control since around 1018, the fact that it was still claimed by the English crown rankled in Scotland. In common with earlier Scottish kings, Malcolm had an ambition to push his frontier south to the River Tyne and, if King Edward had indeed reneged on a promise made in 1059, personal pique may have been an additional spur to action in 1061. Despite being described as the 'sworn brother' of King Edward's protégé Earl Tostig, Malcolm took the opportunity of his absence on pilgrimage to Rome to launch the first of his devastating raids on the hapless Northumbrian population. It was on this occasion that the Scots looted the holy island of Lindisfarne, as noted by Symeon of Durham. However lurid his style, Symeon's dislike of the Scots was not unfounded; no opportunity to plunder was lost and terrible atrocities were committed, and all for no territorial gain whatsoever.

The raid must have caused a serious crisis in the friendship between the 'sworn brothers', and it is said that King Edward himself had to intervene to heal the rift. Peace was, however, restored, and it was with Malcolm that Tostig took refuge while planning his revenge attack on his brother in 1066. And not only Tostig; in the early years of the Conqueror's reign, the Scottish court at Dunfermline became a haven for disaffected English lords and their families. Among them came Margaret, driven by circumstance rather than inclination to be the guest of the Scottish king.

Royal marriages in the medieval period were not contracted, in the first instance, 'for love', and that Margaret represented a glittering prize for Malcolm is without question. His first wife had died around 1067, and as Margaret was descended from every Saxon king of England, marriage with her would strengthen his claim to Lothian, the Anglian portion of his realm. The offence of such an alliance to Norman William I cannot have been lost on Malcolm, but would not have worried him either; he had made his indifference to both Norman and Saxon clear by supporting Tostig, provisioning Harald Hardrada's invasion in 1066 and raiding the north of England with impunity. He may have felt that support for Edgar Ætheling as his brother-in-law would give him a pretext for further invasions and an outside chance of influencing the English succession. That he had also fallen in love with the beautiful, high-minded princess was a bonus. As it dawned on her that she was being 'yearned for', however, Margaret did not instantly return the compliment.

There is no reason to suppose that Margaret's desire for a cloistered life was other than genuine. It seems that she held out against her suitor for some time and that her brother Edgar, who held her fate in his hands, was unwilling to force her into marriage if she found it abhorrent. At the same time, it must have been clear to both of them that a familial connection with the Scottish king could be to Edgar's advantage, and equally clear that they did not have unlimited choice. In the words of the *Anglo-Saxon Chronicle*, 'The king eagerly urged her brother until he said "Yea" to it. And indeed he dared not do otherwise, because they had come into his power'. Malcolm and Margaret were married by Columban rites in the church at Dunfermline, probably after Malcolm came back from his Yorkshire raid in 1070. The ceremony was performed by Fothad, the last 'Celtic' bishop of St Andrews.

It is unhelpful to see the marriage of Malcolm and Margaret as a union between an illiterate oaf and a refined, scholarly princess who happened to fall into his clutches after his first wife died. The best that even his apologists can say for Malcolm is that he was no worse than his contemporaries, but it may be that his actions are more horrifying to modern minds than they were to the woman who married him. Professor A. A. M. Duncan has remarked that 'It is inadequate to characterise tenth- to eleventh-century society as barbarian or primitive, although it had something of both qualities; perhaps the most neutral description is "archaic"'.

It is wise to remember that Margaret was also a product of this archaic society, accepting its values and living by its rules. However refined she was, her scholarship was narrow and, despite the geographical distance she had travelled since childhood, court and cloister were all she knew. She had spent her early years in a country newly and nervously Christian, where lapses from orthodoxy were brutally punished. She belonged to a family where murder and unexplained disappearance were well within living memory. She had passed her adolescence in a land where Viking invasions were far from distant nightmares, and she had been uncomfortably close when the Conqueror landed and one of the great battles of history was fought at Hastings. More recently she had probably been with a rebel army fleeing the wrath of the Normans and, if she did indeed meet Malcolm among the blazing ruins at Wearmouth, she must have understood well enough the nature of the man she had agreed to marry.

It is hard to imagine a more turbulent early life than Margaret's, and easy to comprehend her attraction to the cloister, with its long silences and ordered ways. She may have married to oblige her family, or because her perception of God's will for her had changed, or because union with Malcolm seemed her best chance of the security which inwardly she craved. As a nun or as a queen, Margaret would always be a member of the 'peace-society', those who prayed and nurtured and cared for the dispossessed but, whatever she thought about her husband's table manners, the notion that she abhorred his warlike ways is misplaced. As she assumed the burden of queenship and motherhood, she knew perfectly well that the 'peace-society' she loved was dependent on the 'war-society' which her husband so uncompromisingly represented.

7

COURT
AND COUNTRY

THERE is no doubt that what Margaret experienced in the early days of her marriage was in many respects far removed from the highly cultured, French-influenced corner of England where she spent her adolescent years. Scotland had no equivalent to the richly coloured decoration of the Winchester School, no *opus anglicanum* to fill its churches with candle-reflected gold. The European craze for enriching the church had not yet reached Scotland, nor had Scotland the network of monasteries and nunneries needed to produce the artefacts that made cathedrals like Winchester and Westminster glories of their age. The Viking raids on Iona in the ninth century, causing the removal of many of its treasures to Kells in Ireland, had fatally damaged the church's connection with art; apart from some relics of Columba held at Dunkeld and an undistinguished Gospel book known as *The Book of Deer*, only the beautiful standing stones of the Picts and Scots remained, carved with mysterious symbols which Margaret would neither have recognised nor approved. To understand what Margaret was deprived of is easy, but to visualise the 'palace' which became her first Scottish home needs some imagination, since not a stick of it has survived.

> *For that place was of itself most strongly fortified by nature, being begirt*
> *by very thick woods and protected by steep crags. In the midst thereof was*
> *a fair plain, likewise protected by crags and streams, so that one might*
> *think that this was the spot whereof it was said, scarce man or beast may*
> *tread its pathless wilds.*

This not unattractive description of Dunfermline, *Dun fiar linne* or 'the tower by the crooked stream', is not Turgot's. Turgot's narrative does not mention a single place name, nor describe the Scottish court except in terms of Margaret's improvements to it. The description, from John of Fordun's fourteenth-century chronicle, is true to the nature of the place; even now, after centuries of development and redevelopment, the outline is still discernible.

The implication of Turgot's account – that before its makeover by Margaret the king's house was crude, ill-furnished and lacking in royal finery – may be correct, but only by comparison with the palaces of the Norman French and the West Saxon kings.

By the time Margaret came into his life, Malcolm's first wife, Ingibiorg, had faded from the scene. In the absence of record, various theories about her fate have been aired; that a crisis of conscience due to their supposed consanguinity had led to an annulment of the marriage; that Malcolm, with Margaret in mind, had arranged to have Ingibiorg disposed of. Much more likely is that she died around 1067 of natural causes, leaving the way clear for her husband to marry a woman whose fame would quickly obliterate her. Not much is known about Ingibiorg, but her culture and Malcolm's were compatible, and their dwelling suitable to the place and climate in which they lived.

Although in Germany, at sites such as Magdeburg and Goslar, remains of stone palaces built in the eleventh century have been unearthed, further north wood remained the favoured building material. Archaeological excavations elsewhere prove that the round houses of the Iron Age had largely been superseded, and it is likely that Malcolm's residence was a rectangular timber hall with a central fire-stone, thatched with reeds or straw. Comparisons with the richly furnished great halls of the Irish kings described in the *Ulster Cycle* are fanciful, but it was a substantial structure, with an adjacent chapel and outbuildings consisting of stables, smithy, kitchen, workshops and sleeping quarters for women, servants and men-at-arms. If it was leaky, draughty, insanitary and beached in a sea of mud, it was like most other royal residences in Scandinavia and northern Europe at that time. It was also vastly superior to the dirty, verminous, jerry-built hovels of the common people that clustered around its gates.

All that is known of Margaret's personality suggests that she took seriously the biblical injunction: 'Whatever task lies to your hand, do it with all your might.' She would have been a wholehearted nun, rising in time to be one of the great aristocratic abbesses of her time. Having convinced herself that God had instead called her to be a queen, she threw herself into that role with equal ardour, aided by the rapport which she and Malcolm, the ultimate union of opposites, quickly established. It is essential to remember, however, that as she set out on her mission for change, the new queen had no power to do anything on her own initiative. When Turgot wrote that she was distracted by the 'countless affairs of the kingdom' and that 'all things which became the rule of a prudent queen were done by her; by her advice the laws of the kingdom were administered', he was exaggerating mightily.

Although unlettered, Malcolm was not a fool and he did not abdicate in favour of Margaret. Anything she did was dependent on his authority, and the dynamic of their relationship is the key to everything else. No doubt Margaret's religious fervour touched Malcolm and, being so much older, he showed his affection in almost paternal indulgence. But that their mutual contentment was based on physical compatibility is obvious and, like many powerless women who understood their position, Margaret must often have used 'pillow talk' in an attempt to bring Malcolm round to her point of view. Yet for all his effusive overstatement, Turgot knew the royal household, and it is on the domestic aspect of Margaret's 'reforms' that he is probably most reliable.

There is nothing unusual in a new wife wanting to improve her husband's living quarters. It was the lengths to which Margaret went that now seem extraordinary. It seems that the formerly cloistered young woman suddenly found in herself a taste for the colourful and the exotic. In Turgot's account, she encouraged merchants from England and Europe, who

> *brought with them for sale many and precious kinds of merchandise which in Scotland were before unknown, among which, at the instigation of the queen, the people bought garments of various colours and different kinds of ornaments; so from that time they went about in new costumes of different fashions, from the elegance of which they might be supposed to be a new race.*

This new, glitzy Scotland was, of course, an imaginary one. Although there was commercial expansion in western Europe in the late eleventh century, Margaret would be dead for almost twenty years before ships were recorded as unloading cargo in the Tay. In her lifetime, homespun clothing remained the attire of necessity, if not of choice. Margaret does, however, seem to have sought out purveyors of finery, and no doubt the few who could afford to do so followed her example. She 'walked in state, clad in splendid apparel, as became a Queen', her linen shift or 'sark' topped by a long tunic of fine and brightly dyed wool, its border and sleeves richly embroidered, its belt encrusted with jewels. Over this, as protection against the northern climate, she wore a cloak, fur-lined in winter, fastened at the collar with a gold brooch. Contrary to many depictions of her, however, she did not show her hair; after marriage the plaits of girlhood disappeared under a white linen headcloth, possibly secured with a circlet of gold.

Margaret also

increased the splendour of the royal palace, so that not only was it bright-
ened by the different coloured uniforms worn in it, but the whole house
was made resplendent with gold and silver; for the vessels in which the
king and nobles were served with food and drink were either of gold or
of silver, or gold or silver plated

– this last, presumably, being some small economy. A quaint little book
published in English in 1661 to mark the restoration of the Stuart monarchy
in Charles II, entitled *The Idea of a Perfect Princesse, in the life of St Margaret,*
Queen of Scotland and known as the *Douay Chronicle*, suggests that Margaret
sacked flamboyant cooks and instituted a plain diet at the king's table; this is
more likely to be a retrospective nod to her personal frugality than a reflection
of what was actually set before a group of hungry young aristocrats, whose
diet included beef, venison, game, fish, eggs, nuts and fruit. More famously,
while replacing their receptacles of horn and wood, Margaret also attempted
to tidy up the nobles' table manners. Frowning on the habit of rudely stuffing
down food then bolting from the table without permission, she bribed the
king's companions with extra wine to sit quietly until grace was said.

It seems likely that the queen also frowned on a good deal else as well.
It is hard to imagine her taking kindly to the secular amusements with which
courts diverted themselves during the long winter months – games of chess
and dice, dancing, flirting and listening to the songs and stories of itinerant
minstrels and bards. Margaret's musical education was concentrated on the
Gregorian plainsong of the church, and although there had been a rich tradition of secular music in Europe since the reign of the emperor Charlemagne
in the early ninth century (Anglo-Saxon depictions of 'gleemen' show dancers,
jugglers, trumpeters and cheerful players of stringed instruments), frivolous
entertainment cannot have appealed to her. Perhaps Malcolm, with conflicting
interests to appease, urged compromise in such matters, but what the court
had gained in sumptuousness it may well have lost in jollity. The king did,
however, allow himself to be kitted out in smart new clothes and, whether
walking or riding, he was now attended by a large group of a 'higher class of
servants' whom his wife hired for him.

It is all reminiscent of the English queen Edith who, under the gaze of an
adolescent princess recently arrived from Hungary, decked her elderly, unpretentious husband in embroidered robes, put a jewel-encrusted walking stick
in his hand and bought Spanish carpets for his throne room. It is a modern

perception that Margaret wanted to 'civilise' or 'Normanise' the Scottish court. She was much more intent on enhancing Malcolm's regal status, remaking him in her image of what a powerful monarch should be and thus bolstering her own security and that of her family. That she had learned from Edith's management style, demure in public and plain-speaking behind the scenes, is equally likely. Perhaps Malcolm had learned something from King Edward too; the knack of keeping an enthusiastic young wife onside while reserving absolute power in sovereign affairs.

Not only in the household sphere can Edith's example be detected in Margaret's practice. Just as Edith endowed Wilton Abbey for the good of her soul, Margaret began soon after her marriage to extend the modest church where she had wed Malcolm, dedicating the new structure to the Holy Trinity. It too was provided with precious vessels of silver and gold, and presented with a crucifix 'of incomparable value, having upon it an image of the Saviour which [Margaret] had caused to be covered with a vestment of purest gold and silver studded with gems'. Young women of noble birth and the required degree of gravitas were recruited to learn the *opus anglicanum* (no flirtatious young men, unescorted by the queen, were allowed to intrude on their holy work parties), and Margaret's room filled up with copes, chasubles, stoles, altar-cloths and church ornaments.

It seems that even the admiring Turgot found it hard to reconcile this lust for splendour with the ideal of holy poverty, since he felt obliged to point out, rather defensively, that

> *this the queen did not because the honour of the world delighted her ... though compelled to do the things which are of the world, she deemed it beneath her to set her affections upon them; for she delighted more in good works than in abundance of riches.*

This sounds like a loyal repetition of words he had heard from the queen's own lips, her self-justification for the pride of place and person that was her most striking worldly characteristic. Certainly Turgot would not have been the only monk, in his time, to feel unease at the paradox of a vastly wealthy church, endowed by vastly wealthy people, and the preaching of the virtue of poverty by its founder. St Bernard of Clairvaux, the great Cistercian ascetic born around the time when Turgot was writing, was raging thirty years later against the possession by monks of preposterously bejewelled artefacts; a vast gold candlestick donated to the monastery at Cluny by Margaret's daughter, Queen Matilda of England, drew his particular contempt.

One question which inevitably comes to mind is from where, in a country as notoriously impoverished as Scotland, the money came to pay for such ostentation. That Margaret had wealth of her own is well attested; a share of the aforementioned riches bestowed on her father by King Andrew I of Hungary and King Edward was probably her dowry, and the gifts she gave to Holy Trinity, Dunfermline and to the shrine of St Andrew at Kilrymont (St Andrews) would have come from these sources. It is also feasible that, like queens elsewhere, she received on her marriage some land rents and tax income for her own use – for if the country itself was deemed poor, King Malcolm was not. There would be no Scottish coinage until his son David captured the English mint at Carlisle Castle in 1136, but Malcolm had considerable income in cash, mostly English, and in kind from extensive crown lands. That the royal treasury was enriched by loot taken from the churches of Northumbria is another thought probably more disturbing to a modern than to an eleventh-century conscience.

In the midst of so much business Margaret, like other women of high and low degree, was very frequently pregnant. The dates of birth of her children are unrecorded and in her thirties she may have had unsuccessful pregnancies, but, over a period of some fifteen years, eight babies were born who survived into maturity. At a time when, according to the researches of Professor H. G. Koenigsberger, the mortality rate in Europe was 15-20% in the first year of life and 30% before the age of twenty, this was a remarkable record. Margaret's fecundity is also an indication that, in the prime of life, her own health was robust; in the early Middle Ages, between the ages of twenty and forty, 30% more women died than men, and the death of women by infectious illness and in childbirth far outstripped the loss of men in battle.

Nothing proves more poignantly Malcolm's indulgence of Margaret than his allowing her to give their children names not from his family, but from hers. The eldest, Edward, was named after Margaret's father and her great-uncle, Edmund after her grandfather Edmund Ironside, Æthelred after her great-grandfather, and Edgar after her brother and also her great great-grand-father. All of these, apart from the Ætheling, had been crowned English kings. Of the younger children, Alexander was named after Pope Alexander II, Edith after Margaret's former mentor and great-aunt by marriage, and Mary in honour of the Virgin. David, neither an English nor a Scottish name, may have been given for the Old Testament king or the Welsh saint, but more probably for a son of King Andrew I of Hungary.

Margaret approached child-rearing with the same zeal she applied to every-

thing else. She has had quite recent apologists, but in reality nothing empha-
sises more starkly the gulf between modern and pre-modern thinking than
the treatment of children. No doubt Malcolm saw to it that his sons were
educated in the martial arts; all but Æthelred, who became lay abbot of
Dunkeld, had in adult life their share of fighting to do. Otherwise the
children's education and conduct were regulated by their mother, as complacently described by Turgot:

> She took all heed that they should be well brought up and especially
> trained in virtue. Knowing that it is written, 'He that spareth the rod
> hateth his son,' she charged the governor who had the care of the nursery to
> scold them, and to whip them when they were naughty, as frolicsome
> children will often be. Thanks to their mother's religious care, her children
> surpassed in good behaviour many who were their elders; they were always
> affectionate and peaceable among themselves, and everywhere the younger
> paid due respect to the elder. Thus it was that during the solemnities of the
> Mass, when they went up to make their offerings after their parents, never
> on any occasion did the younger venture to precede the elder, the custom
> being for the elder to go before the younger according to the order of their
> birth.

They would be strange children of any age who were 'always affectionate and
peaceable among themselves', but the description of a mini hierarchy rings
true. Margaret's belief in regal dignity, her quest for obedience and dislike of
disorder made the repressive upbringing of her family inevitable.

> She frequently called her children to her, and carefully instructed them
> about Christ, as far as their age would permit, and she admonished them
> to love him always. 'O, my children,' she said, 'fear the Lord, for they who
> fear him shall lack nothing, and if you love him, he will give you, my dear
> ones, prosperity in this life and everlasting happiness with all the saints.'

It is as impossible to know how much time Margaret's children actually
spent with her as it is to know how much time she spent with her parents in
Hungary long before. The view that most of their care was delegated to others
is backed up by the fact that her elder daughter, although she lived at home
until she was six or seven, called for Turgot's memoir because she had no
recollection of her mother. Margaret's long-range influence is, however,
indisputable. Edgar, Alexander and David, her sons who ruled Scotland
consecutively between 1097 and 1153, were all renowned for their piety and,

in different degrees, liberality to the church, while her elder daughter Edith, when she became queen of England, was devoted to the church and as extravagantly open-handed as her mother.

There was, of course, more to life in the royal household than housekeeping and the rearing of children. Throughout her married life Margaret knew that at any moment her husband might go to war, and that her only recourse was to pray for his safe return. The first trial of this kind was not long in coming. The fact that Margaret's marriage to Malcolm gave their children a claim, however unlikely to be realised, to the English throne had not been lost on William the Conqueror. Nor was he pleased by Malcolm's continued harbouring of English dissidents; although Malcolm had as yet sworn no oath to him, he clearly regarded the Scottish king as too big for his boots. For two years after the wedding, William was busy flushing out malcontents elsewhere, but in 1072, deciding on a show of strength, he moved into Scotland with a large force. At the same time he brought his fleet up the east coast to alarm the Scots and support his army. Even more alarming than the sight of the great, dragon-prowed armada, so reminiscent of the fearsome Vikings from whom the Normans were descended, must have been the sight of a Norman host on the march. Mail-clad, helmeted and armed with swords and lethal spears, their tight ranks bore more resemblance to a Roman army than to the poorly resourced part-timers usually pitted against them. Unchallenged, the Normans forded the Forth above Stirling, penetrating into the Scottish heartland as far as Abernethy. Outside this royal town, the site of a Pictish monastery since around 600, William prepared for battle within sight of his longships at anchor in the Tay.

Knowing of the Normans' advance, Malcolm, who had no standing army, had hastily assembled a force to oppose them. Faced by the steely ranks that had defeated the Saxons at Hastings, however, he decided not to put his soldiers to the test. Envoys were sent to William's camp, and the two kings met to negotiate. The result was that Malcolm knelt before William and, in return for the face-saving gift of a few English manors and an annual pension of twelve marks in gold, swore an oath to be his obedient vassal in the future. As was customary on these occasions, the Scottish king gave hostages as a guarantee of his good faith; these included Duncan, his first son with Ingibiorg. The rules governing the treatment of hostages were strict, and the twelve-year-old would be dealt with kindly enough, housed and educated as became his status as a prince. But he was going alone among people whose language he did not speak, and his use as a pawn by his own father is another indication of how differently children, and in particular royal children, were regarded in the eleventh century. Duncan would live to return to Scotland, but his disjunction from his family was permanent. As a result of the agreement at Abernethy, Edgar Ætheling too was obliged to leave Scotland for Flanders, presumably taking his mother and his unmarried sister with him. Unlike Duncan's, his absence would not be prolonged.

It cannot be known for certain how much of Scotland Margaret actually visited – whether, for instance, she ever saw Iona, which was one of her benefactions. Turgot, with his vague topography and failure of interest in anything beyond court and cloister, gives a claustrophobic impression of a queen enclosed in church and chambers packed with gaudy artefacts, but this may be misleading. Turgot himself mentions in passing that during the last six months of her life Margaret was too ill to ride on horseback, and one senses that this was a deprivation. It is at least arguable that, during her twenty-three years of marriage, she may have ridden far beyond the woods of Fife and the shores of Lothian.

By the time he met King William I at Abernethy, Malcolm had already raided the north of England twice, and would raid it again three times before his death in 1093. Even if the raid of 1091 took longer than the average six weeks, these expeditions did not occupy the king for more than a year. If the time taken to go north to Moray in 1078 and deal with a rebellion instigated by Lulach's son Mael Snechta is added, Malcolm's fighting days still account for no more than fourteen months of his thirty-six year reign. Yet so compelling is his reputation as a warrior king, it is rarely asked what he was doing the rest of the time. The answer, of course, is that he was behaving in a kingly way at home, hunting, practising swordsmanship, dealing with administrative affairs, hearing legal cases and passing judgement – and riding around the country to make his presence felt.

One aspect of Scottish life which must have been perfectly familiar to Margaret was its hierarchical structure – king first, nobility second and below them peasants of various degrees. Status depended on land holding; in the absence of a national coinage, cattle traditionally provided a kind of alternative currency. Under the king, the most important lords were the *mormaers* or 'great stewards', who controlled and dispensed justice in large tracts of the country. These were immensely powerful men who might themselves, through royal kinship, aspire to the throne; Macbeth had been mormaer of Moray before he disposed of his kinsman Duncan I. Further down the scale of power, and much more numerous, were *thanes*, royal officials who administered areas known as shires from centres called *thanages*. Their duties included collecting revenue, managing common resources such as peat banks, mills and pasturage, and organising services and labour due to the king. The majority of the population were peasants, the more fortunate craftsmen and free farmers, who paid for their land in kind and were obliged to do military service at the behest of their overlords. The less fortunate were tied to the land where they worked. Little more than slaves, they were not only obliged to hand over a portion of their miserable produce, but also to do menial tasks like ditching and road maintenance.

The occupation of land in all of Scotland, apart from the province of Lothian with its ties to the English crown, brought with it four obligations to the king or to another superior – usually the church. Two of these involved providing men for military service within Scotland and abroad; the others, 'cain' and 'conveth', were vital to the royal exchequer. 'Cain' was rent due to the king, his right to a share of the land's produce; in arable districts this was traditionally paid in grain, in areas of pasture in cattle or pigs. By the time of Malcolm III cash payments, mostly in English coin, were accepted in lieu. The word 'conveth' derives from an Irish word meaning 'feast'. Based on the ancient right of the leader of a tribe to be supported by his followers, it came to signify a meal and a night's lodging given by occupiers of land to its superior when he visited the district. Legally he might call upon this hospitality four times a year.

This was not, of course, simply a matter of providing the king himself with dinner and a bed for the night. The royal progress, a summer journey around the country with a large retinue, bankrupting one's subjects with demands for extravagant hospitality, was still a favoured means of avoiding personal expenditure in the late sixteenth century. On a practical level, the royal dwelling had to be vacated so that the latrines could be emptied and, if the king had legal and administrative business in distant parts, it made sense to avoid the winter weather. But it was also important, in an age without 'media', for the monarch to be seen, and to be seen impressively supported. Loyalty could not be taken for granted, and Malcolm could not afford to be 'out of sight, out of mind'. It is perfectly feasible that, except in the last stages of pregnancy, Margaret and the older children, along with the procession of retainers, bodyguards and servants she considered suitable to his position, joined Malcolm on his travels. If so, accepting hospitality in houses all over the country, the queen must have learned more about the social and religious condition of Scotland than has sometimes been allowed.

8

MARGARET'S CHURCH

THE claim that Margaret introduced into Scotland Norman customs and religious practices, to the detriment of the indigenous culture, is not only a modern one; the first backlash against perceived Norman influence at court came hot on the heels of Malcolm and Margaret's deaths in 1093. In fact, there had been Normans in Scotland long before Margaret arrived. The first had probably come from Mercia, driven out during King Edward's squabble with the Godwin family in 1051, and Norman mercenaries had fought for Macbeth against Earl Siward in 1054. Until Margaret's time, however, their impact on Scottish lifestyle had been minimal and the culture she represented, with its intertwining of continental and native English elements, is better described as 'Anglo-Norman'. In Scotland it was a courtly phenomenon, and if Margaret made changes in secular life much beyond the palace walls, there is little evidence for them. To concentrate on the alterations she made to court practice, however, is to obscure her larger purpose. What she wanted most passionately was to see change in the church.

The ecclesiastical scene in Scotland clearly came as a terrible shock to Margaret, born a Roman Catholic, reared by Benedictines and by nature a devout and obedient daughter of the church. The conformity of belief and practice that had been imposed in Europe, often at swordpoint by rulers as violent as they were zealous, had barely impinged on a church which, though giving nominal allegiance to Rome, had its roots in a very different tradition. To understand Margaret's relationship with it, it is necessary to consider what she believed and the nature of the institution that affronted her so deeply.

However familiar she was with learned commentaries, Margaret's core beliefs were based on the Gospels, the four New Testament narratives of the life and teachings of Jesus Christ, and on the Rule of St Benedict, itself an interpretation of these teachings. It was the Rule that dictated her structured, prayer-based daily life; her gravity of manner, dislike of hilarity, insistence on serious conversation and long silences all derive from this source.

In a revealing passage that evokes vividly Margaret's impact on her husband's courtiers, Turgot remarks that

> *in her presence no one ventured to do anything wrong, or even to utter an unseemly word .... Always angry with her own faults, she sometimes reproved those of others with that commendable anger tempered with justice which the psalmist enjoined when he said, 'Be angry and sin not'.*

The words 'holy terror' come to mind, and when one reads of Margaret's horror of 'unseemly familiarity and pert frivolity' among the young ladies and gentlemen of the court, it is hard to resist the thought that inside her there was a strict Benedictine abbess trying to get out. But there is no doubt that the injunctions of the Rule and of the Gospel weighed on her heavily, and it was not her fault that she lacked the sardonic sense of humour which helped later generations in Scotland to cope with their alarming beliefs.

Margaret did not live in an age of liberal interpretation of scripture. She believed everything literally and knew no way of shrugging off the darker aspects of her faith. Like Christians down the ages, she was haunted by the passage in Matthew's Gospel (25:31-46) in which the Last Judgement, on the day when the world will come to an end, is described as the separation by Christ of the righteous sheep and the unrighteous goats. Although she lived two hundred years before the Franciscan friar Thomas of Celano wrote the great *Dies Irae* or 'Day of Wrath', the awe-inspiring meditation on death and judgement which entered the liturgy of the church and fed the imaginations of writers, artists and composers well into modern times, Margaret would have been perfectly in tune with its passionate appeal:

> *Among the sheep give me a place*
> *And from the goats sequester me,*
> *Placing me at thy right hand.*
> *When the accursed have been silenced*
> *Given up to bitter flames,*
> *Call me with the blessed.*

The unrighteous were those who had failed in the seven corporal works of mercy codified by St Benedict: to tend the sick; to feed the hungry; to give drink to the thirsty; to clothe the naked; to harbour the stranger; to minister to prisoners; to bury the dead. Margaret took with the utmost seriousness Christ's words of praise for the righteous: 'Anything you did for one of my brothers here, however humble, you did for me.' She believed just as fervently that those who failed the test were bound for hell, a place of real torment and punishment without parole.

St Benedict had also listed seven spiritual works of mercy, to which Margaret applied herself with equal intensity. Most are uncontentious: to comfort those in sorrow; to bear wrongs patiently; to forgive injuries; to pray for the living and the dead. The others – to convert the sinner; to instruct the ignorant; to counsel those in doubt – have overtones unfashionable in a multi-faith society, but Margaret did not live in a multi-faith society. Her objection to the church in Scotland was not that it was unchristian, but that it was not in accordance with the papally governed, doctrinally and ritually homogeneous church of western Europe to which she belonged – and which by all indications she believed to be the whole of Christendom. That the Scottish church should adapt to this model must have seemed obvious to a rigid conformist like Margaret, who saw in her new position of eminence a God-sent opportunity to drive through a programme of change.

Christianity had come to Scotland by two routes. Ninian, who died around 432, was a Briton of Strathclyde, ordained bishop of the southern Picts by Pope Sicurus in 394. He founded the church of Candida Casa (the White House) at Whithorn in Galloway and, according to the Venerable Bede, preached Christianity to the Picts of all southern Scotland as far as the Grampians. He was truly the first missionary, since it was 563 before the Irish aristocrat Columba, also known as Columkille and Colm, sailed from Ulster to found a monastery on the small Hebridean island of Hy, better known as Iona. The island was the base for his chief mission to the Irish Scots who had settled on the Argyllshire coast. Columba and his rapidly expanding band of followers also preached to the Picts, allegedly visiting the court of King Brudei at Inverness, although it is doubtful whether, in Columba's lifetime, they made much impact east of Breadalbane.

Although professing allegiance to Rome since the time of St Patrick (c.385-c.461) the Irish church was an idiosyncratic organisation. It was embedded in a magnificent and deeply spiritual cultural tradition, but its island isolation prevented much intellectual intercourse with the church elsewhere. Its off-shoot in Scotland was for a time very successful and in 635 Aidan, a monk of Iona, went at the invitation of King Oswald of Northumbria (605-41) to establish a monastery on Lindisfarne, the Holy Island. The saintly Cuthbert (c.635-87) was resident there, and after his death one of the great Celtic works of art, the illuminated manuscript known as the Lindisfarne Gospels, was created in his memory. Many converts were made in Northumbria and Mercia, but the flowering of the Celtic church in England was short-lived. In 596 Pope Gregory I had dispatched a Roman cleric, Augustine (?-c.604) with forty monks on a mission to England. Landing the following year, Augustine was well received (the queen was already a Christian and King Ethelbert of Kent kindly disposed), established his headquarters at Canterbury and was soon consecrated bishop of the English. It was only a matter of time before his Roman, southern church came into conflict with the Celtic church of Columba in the north.

The clash came at the Synod of Whitby in 664. After a bruising encounter between Colman of Iona and Wilfrid, a Lindisfarne-educated monk who had gone over to the side of Rome, it was decided to adopt throughout England the Latin rites and Roman practices prevalent throughout western Europe. Humiliated by their defeat, the Celtic monks were obliged to leave their monastery on Lindisfarne to the Romanists and withdraw, first to Iona and subsequently to Ireland. The church in Scotland, left to its own devices, became even more isolated and out of step with the rest of Europe. Its influence declined, and far from being a slightly eccentric but thriving establishment, by the time of Margaret it was a shambles. Church attendance was irregular and many of the clergy, almost all of whom belonged to a group known as 'Culdees' (a corruption of the Gaelic *Céli De*, meaning 'Vassals of God'), lived in loosely knit communities at sites like St Andrews, Brechin, Monymusk and Dunkeld, wearing secular clothes, marrying and owning personal property. Others lived as hermits, devoting themselves to prayer and dependent for their meagre food on the charity of others.

It has never been seriously suggested that Margaret disliked or despised the Scottish clergy in any personal way. She had been married by the Culdee bishop Fothad and she admired the hermits, seeking them out for prayerful advice and giving money to good causes which they advocated. She endowed the shrine of St Andrew and, in association with Malcolm, granted land to Culdee monasteries at Loch Leven and Monymusk. Nor is there any evidence that she objected to her son Æthelred being given the sinecure of the lay abbacy of Dunkeld, although there her silence may simply have been tactful; Malcolm's grandfather Crinan had held the same position, while her own grandfather, Count Bruno of Brunswick, had been a bishop before the rules on clerical celibacy began to be tightened up by Rome. The fact remains that, in Margaret's eyes, the church in Scotland was seriously out of kilter with the 'universal' church and, in her eyes, ripe for reform.

Turgot remarks, in his awestruck fashion, that Margaret enjoyed debate with learned men, meaning clerics, of whom she asked 'profound questions'. The motif of the youthful scholar confounding his elders with superior wisdom had been recurrent in religious literature since biblical times, and the response to Margaret was the familiar one: 'As among them no one had a profounder intellect ... it often happened that these teachers left her much more learned than when they came.' Perhaps these alleged triumphs emboldened Margaret to ask Lanfranc (c.1005-89), the Italian-born, French-educated lawyer, schoolmaster and Benedictine monk who had recently become Archbishop of Canterbury, to be her spiritual adviser. That Lanfranc was flattered is evident from the fulsome tone of his reply, the sole surviving remnant of their correspondence.

> *Lanfranc, unworthy bishop of the holy church of Canterbury to the most glorious queen of the Scots, Margaret, greeting and benediction .... It has come that thou, born of royal stock, royally brought up and united to a noble king, hast chosen me, a stranger, worthless, ignoble and tangled in sin ....*

It is unlikely, however, that Lanfranc was greatly in awe of Margaret's intellectual prowess; he was himself a formidable scholar and also – interestingly in the complex flow of Anglo-Scottish relations – the Conqueror's appointee and one who claimed Canterbury's superiority over all other churches in mainland Britain.

Margaret's sense of loss when she discovered that there were no Benedictine foundations in Scotland was understandable. So, given her determination to sort out the peculiarities of Scottish monastic life, was her desire to plant in her husband's realm communities of the orthodox, disciplined religious whom she trusted and admired. It was partly in response to her request for Benedictine monks from Canterbury to come to Dunfermline that Lanfranc penned his letter, but, despite its unctuous tone, its lukewarm commitment must have disappointed Margaret.

> *According to thy request, I send to thy glorious husband and thee our dearest brother, sir Goldwine; also two other brothers ... and if you can, or wish to, fulfil your work through others, we would greatly desire that these our brothers should return to us.*

The most that can be said is that a small Benedictine community was established at Dunfermline in Margaret's lifetime and that Turgot, who claimed to have had charge of the gold and silver altar vessels at the church of the Holy Trinity and to have been the queen's confessor, may for a short period have been a member of it.

The 'frequent councils' which, says Turgot, Margaret convened to thrash out her differences with the Scottish clergy are much more difficult to set in a historical context. That some disputation between Margaret and 'learned men' did take place is likely, given the strength of her opinions, and the detail that Malcolm had to interpret for her because she did not speak Gaelic is interesting. But whether such meetings were formal is questionable; places and dates are unrecorded and, in the absence of any other mention of them, they probably owe more to the hagiographer's perception of spiritual truth than to actual events. But since Turgot, writing of the 'most important' council, has Margaret deal with the points which really did separate the Scottish church from that in the rest of western Europe, his account is worth considering – while keeping in mind that the thorns in her flesh were still thorns in his when, as Benedictine bishop of St Andrews, he was complaining of them to Pope Paschal II in 1114.

The 'five points of difference', no doubt a summary of the deviations that most vexed Margaret and Turgot, were these:

1. That the Scottish church began Lent (the period of fasting preceding Easter) not on Ash Wednesday but on the first Monday following, thus cutting the fast from forty days to thirty-six.
2. That the Holy Sacrament of Communion was not celebrated on Easter Day.
3. That Mass in some places was celebrated with a 'barbarous ritual' contrary to the custom of the universal church.
4. That the 'Lord's Day' was not respected because the Scots worked on Sundays.
5. That marriage was permitted by the Scottish church within the forbidden degrees of relationship.

In the face of these charges, the response of those representing the Scottish position was unsurprisingly muted; the Scots have frequently bowed to the prevailing wind before quietly carrying on as usual. In answer to the first claim, they pointed out that in the matter of fasting they acted on the authority of scripture, fasting like Christ in the wilderness for six weeks. In her role as 'a second Helena' (the mother of Constantine, first Christian emperor of Rome, who reputedly confounded the Jews with her scriptural arguments), Margaret riposted that since it was not the custom of the church to fast on Sundays, the four days lost in this calculation must be added to the previous week. Silenced by the queen's superior arithmetic, the Scots gave way.

The next point, in the context of Scottish experience, is more resonant. When asked by Margaret why, unlike everyone else, the Scots did not take Communion on Easter Day, the reply was that they felt themselves unworthy to do so. The clerics justified their stance by quoting the admonition of St Paul (c.10-c.66) to the church at Corinth: 'Anyone who eats the bread or drinks the cup of the Lord unworthily, will be guilty of desecrating the body and blood of the Lord', or, in the 1611 Authorised Version of the Bible's even more frightening translation, 'eateth and drinketh damnation to himself, not discerning the Lord's body' (1 Corinthians 2:27-29). That this defence was beyond Margaret's comprehension is understandable; it has always seemed bizarre to Christians whose beliefs are not attuned to the Scottish sensibility. Well into the twentieth century, especially in the Highlands and the Hebrides, elderly adherents of the Free and Free Presbyterian churches, lifelong attenders of Communion services but deeply convinced of their own sinfulness, shrank from taking the Sacrament due to their horror of these words. Even in less fundamentalist Presbyterian congregations they caused a frisson, making the twice-yearly Communion Sunday a solemn and portentous occasion. Margaret's impatient reply, that if sinners were excluded there would be no Communion at all, was the standard response to Scottish scruples down the ages by those who simply could not understand them. Turgot has the Scots bowing to Margaret's superior reasoning, but such visceral beliefs are not so easily changed.

There has been much discussion as to the nature of the 'barbarous ritual' of which Margaret disapproved. Probably it was no more than the use of Gaelic rather than Latin in church services. This would have been particularly irritating to Margaret if it is true that she never mastered Gaelic – an odd failure in a linguist who lived among Gaelic-speaking people for more than twenty years. If this is the correct interpretation of the phrase, Margaret failed to impose her preference; the Culdees were still celebrating Mass in the vernacular half a century later, during the reign of her son David I.

'Let us,' Turgot has Margaret say, 'venerate the Lord's Day, because on it our Saviour arose from the dead,' backing up her plea with a quotation from a letter of Pope Gregory I, in which he rebukes and excommunicates a man who has done a piece of work on Sunday, the Christian day of rest. The Scots were in fact following the practice of the Irish church, which observed the Jewish Sabbath, Saturday, as the God-sanctioned day of rest: 'God blessed the seventh day and made it holy, because on that day he ceased from all the work he had set himself to do' (Genesis 2:3). In the *Life of St Columba* by Adomnán, ninth abbot of Iona, Columba addresses his servant Dairmid, on the last Saturday of his life:

> *This day in the holy scriptures is called the Sabbath, which means rest, and this day is indeed a Sabbath to me, for it is the last day of my present laborious life. This night at midnight which commences the solemn Lord's Day, I shall go the way of our fathers.*

A reasoned point of view, but once again, in Turgot's version, Margaret's assertion that the day of Christ's resurrection should take precedence over Jehovah's rest-day gave her an easy triumph over the rustic Scots.

> *Unable to contradict those arguments of the wise Queen, they henceforth at her insistance observed the Lord's Day with such reverence that no man dared to carry a burden on it, nor did any man venture to compel another to do so.*

And so on, with Margaret crushing opposition to 'abuses' and 'abominable practices' such as the marriage of a man with his stepmother or a widow with her deceased husband's brother, and her audience meekly 'laying aside their obstinacy' and 'willingly undertaking to adopt whatever she desired'. Even those who admire Margaret must admit that she emerges from this narrative as cocksure and smug, and it is a relief to think that, although these were no doubt her opinions, the unpleasant confrontation described by Turgot is unlikely to have taken place. It is also sadly evident that if the Scottish clergy were out of touch with the wider church, so was she. Only thirty years before she took it upon herself to instruct the 'learned men' of Scotland, the Roman and eastern Orthodox branches, after two centuries of bickering over points of doctrine and ritual hardly more momentous than those that riled Margaret, had parted in a schism so bitter, far-reaching and permanent as to make the aberrations of the Scottish church very small beer indeed.

If it were ever proved that Edward Ætheling was reared in the eastern Orthodox faith, an ironic footnote would be added to the life story of his elder daughter. Leaving that issue aside, it still seems strange, considering the network of contacts and relationships known to have existed among European royal houses and the tendency of news to travel, that Margaret should have arrived in Scotland completely unaware that the church she belonged to was not, in fact, the 'universal church'. Perhaps her Benedictine convent education really had made her so insular and narrowly focused that she had no idea what was happening elsewhere. Or perhaps she equated dissent with the disorder she hated so much, and had buried the rumours she had heard in a dark recess of her mind, along with other things she found too disturbing to recall.

It is obvious that Malcolm III loved his wife and was anxious to indulge her as far as he possibly could. He had declared his sensitivity to the issue of the independence of the Scottish church in 1074, when he expelled Aldwin and Turgot from Melrose, yet he had given Turgot access to his household and even allowed Margaret to associate with Lanfranc, whose expressed wish was to draw Scotland into a diocesan system under the authority of Canterbury. Delivering the church she wanted was, however, beyond even a king's power. On a personal level, although to please her he may superficially have become more observant of religious rites, helping Margaret with lenten rituals such as feeding beggars and washing the feet of the poor, there is no evidence of any real spiritual conversion. Malcolm's benefactions, even jointly with his wife, were few and, in spite of Margaret's reputation, during his reign Scotland was virtually absent from the European Christian consciousness. In *The Kingship of the Scots 842-1292*, Professor A. A. M. Duncan points out that Malcolm took no recorded interest in the churches of his kingdom. Tellingly, Pope Gregory VII, whose pastoral concern for marginal countries like Norway, Sweden and Ireland was expressed through correspondence with their kings, did not send a single letter to Malcolm.

So did Margaret's zeal for reform make any real difference to the church in Scotland, given that in her own lifetime her success in changing it was far more limited than was once believed? The answer is that if she is seen as a sower rather than a reaper, she had a posthumous victory. It has often been pointed out that Margaret's greatest contribution to Scotland was the production of kingly sons who shared her religious values, and it was during their reigns that the things she had worked and prayed for would happen at last.

9

THE QUEEN'S
BROTHER

I T is not known exactly when the fortress on the rock at Edinburgh became
a favoured residence of Malcolm and Margaret, nor much about its development prior to their occupation. The early history of the site is poorly
recorded; despite much evidence of prehistoric settlement in the surrounding
area, there is little of occupation of the castle rock itself, and the earlier Roman
invaders of Scotland seem to have passed it by. It has been tentatively identified as *alata castra*, the 'winged fort' mentioned in a list of settlements not
marked but appended to the Latinised version of Ptolemy's second-century
map of Britain, because of its alleged similarity to a great bird in flight.
By the seventh century it had acquired the name *Din Eidyn*, which simply
means 'the fortress of the hill slope'. The association of the name with the
Northumbrian king Edwin, who was dead before his Anglic subjects captured
the site in 638, is now believed to be erroneous. The substitution of *burh*,
the Anglo-Saxon equivalent of the Celtic *dun*, meaning a fortification, dates
from that time. Over the years, a narrow town of thatched wooden houses
formed along the rocky spine bisecting the marshland to north and south,
making an informal capital for the province of Lothian.

The reason for Malcolm and Margaret's predilection for the high, wind-
raked, wooden-walled fortress is obscure. It seems that, before his marriage
to Margaret, Malcolm had used the place as a hunting lodge, a base for expeditions into the great forest of Drumselch which then extended to the south
and east. It has been suggested that Margaret found its Anglian milieu more
congenial than that of Gaelic-speaking Dunfermline less than twenty miles
away, and also that, as he became more involved in the affairs of his brother-
in-law Edgar Ætheling, Malcolm found it a convenient base for military
operations. Perhaps the bleak, exposed situation, close to the elements in which
our ancestors sensed the presence of God, appealed to the ascetic in Margaret,
although the dark, draughty rooms must also have challenged her skills
as an interior decorator. There are traditional accounts of the magnificent

apartment she created for herself at Edinburgh, and a suggestion that she gathered there the young ladies who were learning the *opus anglicanum*, but nothing more. Not a trace of eleventh-century building survives on the castle rock; even the famous oratory, long believed to have been Margaret's own, is now tentatively dated 1128. Nor is there any evidence to support the supposition that it was built on the site of an earlier chapel used by her, although it would have been in character for Margaret to establish a place of prayer close to her living-quarters.

All that can be said for certain is that, at some time during Malcolm and Margaret's marriage, the former hunting lodge became the residence that would later be associated with them as strongly as Dunfermline. The two places were within easy reach of each other, using the Forth crossing subsequently called 'Queensferry' to commemorate the free passages which Margaret established for pilgrims travelling to the shrine of St Andrew in Fife. If it is true that the affairs of the Ætheling weighed at all in Malcolm's decision to establish a household at Edinburgh, a later date in his reign suggests itself, since until the late 1080s he had managed to avoid serious involvement in Edgar's troubled career.

The banishment of Edgar Ætheling from Scotland after the pact of Abernethy did not last long. Only two years later, while King William was in Normandy, the young man reappeared at the Scottish court from Flanders, presumably with his mother and sister in tow. Christina did not become a nun at Romsey until 1086, when it is likely that her two nieces, Edith and Mary, went south with her to begin their convent education. Since Edith could not have been more than six and Mary was even younger, it is not surprising that they grew up with little memory of their mother. There is no contemporary reference to back up the *Douay Chronicle's* assertion that Agatha decided to join Christina in the convent, though it is a probable enough end for an aristocratic widow. Even more probable is that she was still travelling around with Edgar in 1074, when she would not have been much over fifty.

While he was in Scotland Edgar received a letter which must have excited him considerably; it came from King Philip I of France, and contained an offer of tenancy of the castle at Montreuil, the small port between Flanders and Normandy which guarded the only French exit to the sea. The offer was made, according to the *Anglo-Saxon Chronicle*, so that Edgar might 'daily annoy [the king's] enemies', meaning the Conqueror; Philip had not forgiven his former vassal for becoming a king like himself. Ever the opportunist, Edgar accepted and, whether or not Margaret approved of her brother's defection from King William, to whom he had sworn an oath of allegiance, nothing speaks more eloquently of her sisterly love than the generosity of Edgar's send-off to his new appointment.

'King Malcolm and his sister Margaret,' continues the *Chronicle*, 'gave him and his men great presents and many treasures; skins ornamented with purple, pelisses made of marten, miniver and ermine, robes of purple and vessels of gold and silver'. Then, having made sure that Edgar was suitably provisioned for his new position, they 'conducted him and his crew in great pomp from [the king's] territory'. Unfortunately, things had a habit of not going right for Edgar. As he and his companions were sailing down the east coast of England, the sky grew dark and

> *there came upon them such rough weather, and the strong winds and stormy sea drove them so violently onto the shore that all their ships burst, and they also themselves came with difficulty to land. Their treasure was nearly all lost, and some of [Edgar's] men were taken by the Normans. But he himself and his best men returned again to Scotland, some roughly travelling on foot and some miserably mounted.*

It must have been a sorry procession that trudged damply through the courtyard at Dunfermline into the presence of a famously irascible king.

When he agreed to Malcolm's marriage to Margaret, Edgar had no doubt harboured hope that his brother-in-law would 'daily annoy' the English king on his behalf, but Malcolm had not committed himself. Now he advised Edgar to settle his differences with King William; the advice was taken and the Conqueror, with his usual mysterious forbearance towards the Ætheling, graciously received his overtures. Malcolm and Margaret kitted Edgar out almost as sumptuously as before and he again departed, though not this time by sea. On his journey south he was met at Durham by the sheriff of York, who conducted him all the way to Normandy, and there he again did homage to King William. Virtually landless until now, Edgar was granted adequate estates in Hertfordshire and given a pension of one pound of silver per day. It is likely that, at the same time, the Conqueror conferred on Christina the estates in Warwickshire and Oxfordshire which are listed under her name in the *Domesday Book*. Thus, belatedly, some modest compensation was made by the Normans to the children of Edward Ætheling.

If Malcolm and Margaret heaved sighs of relief at Edgar's departure, no one could blame them. With Edgar settled, they could commit themselves to the affairs of state, domestic and devotional life which separately concerned them. It was 1079 before Malcolm decided to break seven years of peace with King William by again invading Northumbria. The reason for this major incursion is obscure but, with William away in Normandy, it may have been no more than a cattle-raid like those described in the *Ulster Cycle*, by which Irish kings provided an outlet for the pent-up energies of their aggressive young followers – and rewarded loyalty at no cost to themselves. Symeon of Durham, implacable as ever, records the slaughter and the taking of booty by the king of Scots, 'a man of the greatest ferocity and with a bestial disposition', while Ailred of Rievaulx, unsparing of the dreadful details but as usual more conciliatory to the Scots, notes that amid the carnage Malcolm spared the church at Hexham 'through honour for the saints who rest in it'. It is hard to resist the suspicion that fear of trouble back home had some bearing on this act of pious restraint.

It was 1080 before King William responded, sending his eldest son Robert, known as 'Curthose' or 'Short-boots', north with an army, which penetrated Scotland as far as Falkirk. In a repetition of the earlier stand-off at Abernethy, Malcolm declined to fight and Robert, who got on well with him personally, decided not to press the matter. After negotiation, Malcolm did homage to Robert as William I's heir, the Abernethy agreement was renewed and hostages were again given as a guarantee of the Scottish king's good behaviour. On his way south, however, Robert stopped long enough to supervise the erection of a castle on the Tyne, subsequently called the 'Newcastle'. This may have been to appease his father, who would have preferred a more heavy-handed resolution, or to warn the Northumbrians, who had recently murdered their Norman-appointed earl. If it was a shot across the bows of the Scots, it was as usual ignored.

Meanwhile the Ætheling, though at last pursuing a life of his own, had not gone for good. Until the last year of King William's life, Edgar remained a member of his household, assuming the fashions and habits of a Norman gentleman and striking up a close friendship with Robert Curthose. Only in 1086 did boredom apparently get the better of him, and he left William's court piqued, says the *Anglo-Saxon Chronicle*, because 'he did not have much honour from him'. In one of the spurts of activity that punctuated the torpid life described by William of Malmesbury, the Ætheling got permission to lead a company of two hundred knights to Apulia in southern Italy, another land under Norman rule. Just what he did there is a mystery, but in any case the adventure did not last long.

In 1087 King William died in Normandy of a wound received while sacking the French town of Mantes. He was succeeded as duke of Normandy by Robert Curthose, and as king of England by his third (second surviving) son William Rufus, so called on account either of his red hair or his florid face. The Conqueror's youngest son, Henry, was given considerable wealth in lieu of land and position. Returning from Italy a year later, Edgar sought out his best friend in Normandy; Duke Robert received him warmly, granting him lands and showing him great favour. The Ætheling might have settled down permanently at Duke Robert's court had he not, through yet another stroke of bad luck, been caught up in an unpleasant family quarrel.

William the Conqueror had disliked his eldest son, who had once assaulted and wounded him. He had wished to leave Normandy as well as England to William Rufus, but had been dissuaded by the nobility of the duchy who wished Robert no ill and had sworn oaths of allegiance to him. Unsurprisingly, the division of spoils pleased no one; Robert wanted England, Rufus wanted Normandy, and a discontented Henry wanted to play one off against the other. A projected invasion of England by Robert, thwarted, says the *Anglo-Saxon Chronicle*, by loyal Englishmen who guarded the sea, was followed in 1090 by an English invasion of Normandy. After much posturing and squabbling, the brothers came to terms at Rouen. Possessions changed hands and it was agreed that each should become the other's heir, but Robert really lost out in the negotiations. Perhaps the most painful of his concessions was his agreement to take back the lands he had given to Edgar Ætheling, and to expel his friend from the country. It has been suggested that William Rufus feared the propaganda value to Robert of his closeness to the Anglo-Saxon claimant, but if so, he gained nothing from trying to break up the relationship. Yet while the return of the disconsolate Edgar to Scotland may well have been the trigger for Malcolm's resumption in 1091 of hostilities against the Norman king, the underlying reasons were more complex.

By advising his brother-in-law to make peace with the Conqueror in 1074, Malcolm had tacitly admitted that by then the Ætheling's claim to the English throne was moonshine. While seventeen years later he might have wished to show solidarity with Margaret's brother – whether egged on by her we shall never know – he would not have gone to war for that alone. R. L. G. Ritchie suggests that, from Edgar's account of his treatment in Normandy, Malcolm guessed that William Rufus was about to demand homage from him; although at Falkirk in 1080 he had submitted to Robert Curthose as William I's heir, Malcolm had so far made no promises to the king's younger son. It is possible too that Malcolm had become alarmed by the growth of Norman power in the north, and the insult to the Ætheling lent some moral force to an invasion which he had already contemplated. In 1091, accompanied by Edgar, he invaded Northumbria for the fourth time, penetrating as far as Chester-le-Street, just north of Durham.

Ancient sources differ as to what happened next. One account in William of Malmesbury's *Historia regum* states that the Scots were sent packing by a single company of English knights, but Symeon of Durham suggests a longer engagement. According to him, while the citizens barricaded themselves inside the gates, the nobility and young men of Durham camped to the south in readiness to defend the city from the Scots on its northern side. From this impasse they were saved by the miraculous intervention of St Cuthbert, who obligingly frightened the Scots into flight. On balance, it seems unlikely that a prolonged seige took place and, whatever the reason for Malcolm's withdrawal, probable that the Scots and their booty were back home before William Rufus, informed in Normandy of their invasion, decided that the time had come to teach their overweening king a lesson.

United for the moment, King William Rufus and Duke Robert returned to England. Using the tactics employed by their father in 1070, they organised a fleet and a massive land army. On this occasion the fleet was wrecked off the coast of Northumbria a few days before Michaelmas (29 September), but meantime the army, headed by Rufus and Robert, had reached Durham. They then pressed on into Lothian, where Malcolm had assembled a force to repel them. According to Orderic Vitalis, the English had penetrated as far as the south bank of the Forth when messengers came sailing across from Malcolm on the other side. Once again he was refusing to fight and, true to form, a deal was brokered between the two kings by their representatives, this time Duke Robert for his brother and Edgar Ætheling for the king of Scots.

It was all *déja vu*. While the Scots watched the steely English army from their positions between Dunfermline and the river, Malcolm did homage to William Rufus, gave hostages and, says the chronicler John of Worcester, was confirmed in the possession of twelve English vills (small areas of land containing one or more settlement) which he had held under the Conqueror. He was also allocated an annual pension of twelve marks of gold, which may have been intended to provide for him on journeys between Scotland and the English court. It is possible too that a marriage between the English king and Malcolm's elder daughter Edith was discussed – although Rufus was thirty-six and Edith only eleven, such an age gap was considered irrelevant in the arrangement of dynastic alliances. Indeed Malcolm, ever eager to secure his border and expand his influence, had already explored the possibility of marrying Edith to Alan the Red, Count of Richmond, an elderly widower who was one of the greatest landowners in the north of England. This plan allegedly came to grief when Alan, having gone to Wilton to inspect Edith, scandalously abducted her schoolmate Gunnhildr, the youngest daughter of the late king, Harold Godwinsson.

Robert and Edgar had reason to feel pleased with themselves. When William Rufus returned south, they went with him, staying at court until Christmas when, with Edgar back in possession of his estates in Normandy, they crossed the Channel together. Edgar had, wisely as things transpired, sought reconciliation with Rufus; all the future he had was dependent on Norman goodwill. That goodwill between Rufus and Malcolm was fragile is made clear by the *Anglo-Saxon Chronicle's* lugubrious comment: 'The kings parted in great friendship, but that lasted only a short time.'

Even English chroniclers, usually so censorious, do not heap blame on Malcolm for what happened next. In the spring of 1092, William Rufus again marched north with a large force, this time to seize Carlisle and drive out Dolfin, the local ruler. Dolfin is thought to have been the son of Cospatric, and so related to the Scottish king, but there is no evidence that, as long believed, he was Malcolm's appointee – or indeed that in 1092 Cumbria was still under the jurisdiction of the Scots. Like his father before him, however, Dolfin fled to Scotland, leaving Rufus to fortify the town, build a great castle and import southern peasants to till the hinterland and supply the garrison.

These actions have been widely regarded as a deliberate provocation of Malcolm and he did protest, but was not sufficiently riled to retaliate. The principal grievance that he nursed against Rufus throughout the following year was of a more personal nature; the English king had failed to grant him the vills he had promised, or to pay him the agreed twelve marks of gold. Malcolm had been hit in his pocket, and it was about this that he complained to William Rufus in the summer of 1093. Rufus, whose own grievances had doubtless been exacerbated by his sense that Malcolm had made a fool of him by refusing to fight in 1091, responded by inviting the complainer to meet him at Gloucester. The haughty expectation that he would travel so far into Rufus's territory, instead of having a kingly conference half way, could scarcely have pleased Malcolm but, by now over sixty and perhaps feeling his age, he agreed. Hostages were given by Rufus as a guarantee of the Scottish king's safe return and, with an irony that cannot have been lost on Malcolm, Edgar Ætheling was sent to Edinburgh, as Rufus's representative, to escort him south.

It is recorded that on 11 August 1093 Malcolm was in Durham where, along with the bishop, William of Calais, and the prior, Margaret's friend Turgot, he laid the foundation stones of a new cathedral. Probably at Margaret's prompting, he also made an agreement with the monks of Durham that they would undertake to say Masses for the welfare of the souls of Malcolm, Margaret and their children, in return for the restoration of lands in Lothian taken from the see of St Cuthbert by the Scottish crown. These pious acts concluded, Malcolm rode south to Gloucester and his meeting with William Rufus, 'a hearty solicitor for peace,' admits William of Malmesbury, 'but only upon just conditions'.

That these conditions were denied him is an understatement. Rufus, who had been seriously ill during Lent but had now recovered, refused point-blank to meet Malcolm, leaving court functionaries to convey to him an ultimatum; he must submit his grievance to the judgement of an English court, or return home empty-handed. The humiliation of such a snub was more than a proud man like Malcolm could bear. To make matters even worse, he heard that Rufus, on his way to Gloucester, had stopped at the convent school at Wilton, where the Scottish princesses now were, to assess the suitability of Edith as a wife – and that the abbess, to save the thirteen-year-old from such a terrible fate, had disguised her as a nun. The probability that such an impudent if well-intentioned trick had fuelled Rufus's animosity against him must have maddened Malcolm, especially if a marriage between Edith and the English king had been seriously discussed two years before.

Stopping only at Wilton to remove his daughter, Malcolm rode back home in a blind fury, having, remarks William of Malmesbury, 'obtained nothing more than permission to return uninjured to his kingdom, for [William Rufus] disdained to take a man by guile whom he might have conquered by arms'. Such contemptuous treatment by a man half his height and almost half his age, whose claim to the throne of England he barely acknowledged, clearly goaded Malcolm beyond endurance. By the time he reached Edinburgh winter was at hand, and the stage was set for a tragedy.

IO

LAST DAYS

NOTHING indicates more starkly Margaret's real powerlessness than her absence from the scenes where the important events of Malcolm's reign took place, and decisions made that affected her safety and the destiny of her children. She must have been at Dunfermline or at Edinburgh when the stand-off on the Lothian shore was resolved, almost close enough to hear the war drums and quite close enough to feel the tension of armies anticipating battle, but she was no more able to influence events than she had been in 1068 when Edgar Ætheling rebelled against William the Conqueror. Posterity has talked up Margaret's power over Malcolm, but one has no sense that when he decided to raid Northumbria, parley with Norman kings or arrange a loveless marriage for his daughter, her views – however eloquently expressed in private – mattered to him one way or another. They were clearly fond of each other, and it is nowhere suggested that Malcolm had amorous interests outside his marriage. But their spheres were separate and, as a woman of her time schooled in the notion of hierarchy, Margaret herself is likely to have accepted this. Nonetheless, with her older sons away from home learning martial arts in the households of Malcolm's allies and her young daughters given over to the care of her austere and – by Edith's own account – far from kindly sister, she must have turned ever more fervently to the religion that was both her burden and her solace.

As described by Turgot, Margaret's daily life was a punishing round of spiritual reading, prayer, fasting and good works, beginning before dawn and ending only briefly at sunset – a replication of the ordered conventual practice to which she remained devoted long after she had accepted that her destiny lay elsewhere. Her Benedictine training had taught her the sinfulness of time wasting, yet the wonder remains that as queen she actually contrived to live the life that the Cluniac reformers of St Benedict's Rule had declared impossible, taking on herself the full burden of the contemplative and the workload of the lay person active in the world. She was up most of the night performing the Benedictine offices, and part of every day was spent in study and prayer, yet somehow she managed to fit in the most extraordinary amount of activity – the management of two households; the choice of clothes and furnishings; the supervision of building work; the *opus anglicanum*; charitable acts; hours on horseback; visits to shrines and hermitages; discussing theology; spending time with the king and overseeing the upbringing of her growing family, while almost constantly pregnant. It has been said of Margaret that she had no sense of proportion; to her one thing was as important as any other, and certainly the impression is of someone who never deputised or shared responsibility, who concentrated her personal attention on every detail, however small. She must have been blessed with an excellent constitution and, as the years passed, have possessed a steely capacity to push her body against the odds. Her robust health was not, however, destined to last for ever.

There is an interesting story concerning Margaret in a *Life* of St Laurence, written about 1095 by Goscelin de Bertin, a Flemish monk then in residence at Canterbury. To Laurence, the seventh-century successor of St Augustine and allegedly a missionary to north-east Scotland, was dedicated the church at Fordoun, near present-day Laurencekirk, and also a church near East Fortune in East Lothian which R. L. G. Ritchie identifies as the site of the 'Margaret' incident. In spite of a ruling, supposedly made by St Laurence himself, that women should be barred from the sanctuary, one day Margaret arrived bearing gifts and determined to lay them in person on the altar. When the monks who had charge of the church flapped out into the courtyard and tried to prevent her from entering, her exasperation with what she no doubt saw as another aberrant Scottish practice boiled over. Telling them haughtily that she had come to honour the saint and exalt the church, she pushed past them, but before she could set foot in the sanctuary she

> *suddenly was seized with severe pains in her whole body, and she said to her retainers, 'Quick, get me out of here! I am dying!' Hastily they brought her outside, and she begged the clerics to intercede for her, and blamed herself for not having heeded their warning.*

This tale is both exemplary and misogynistic, and might be dismissed as a legend but for the date when it was written. 1095 was only two years after Margaret's death, and the incident is described in the text as having occurred 'recently', which means that it must have happened towards the end of her life. Its credibility lies in the fact that, with so many of her immediate family and friends still around, it could easily have been contradicted, but was not. To those who do not believe in such dramatic displays of supernatural displeasure, it might seem that Margaret's seizure, after a long, hard ride, was really evidence that all was not well with her. This interpretation is even more plausible when set alongside other clues to her physical state as Malcolm's long reign drew towards its close.

The exact dates of birth of Margaret and Malcolm's eight children are not known, but it seems that successful pregnancies became less frequent after the birth of Edith around 1080, and ceased with the birth of David when Margaret was about thirty-eight.

The average age of menopause in the eleventh century was forty-five. It is possible that some female ailment such as prolapse of the uterus or pelvic inflammatory disease contributed to the pain and tiredness which Turgot says afflicted Margaret in later life. Alternatively, she may have been suffering from cancer or a debilitating infection unconnected with the bearing of children. But whatever ailed her, her suffering was severely exacerbated by a chronic failure to eat.

When writing his Rule, St Benedict, with his usual disapproval of religious excess, was specific about sensible eating. The flesh of four-footed animals was forbidden to all but the very weak and the sick, but otherwise prohibitions were few. He wrote:

> *For the daily meal, both at the sixth and the ninth hour, two kinds of food are sufficient, so that he who perhaps cannot eat of one may make his meal of the other. Let two kinds of cooked food, therefore, be sufficient ... and if there be fruit and fresh vegetables, a third may be added. Let a pound of bread be sufficient for the day, whether there be only one meal or both dinner and supper. If they are to eat supper, let a third part of the pound be reserved by the cellarer and given at supper.*

Although Benedict approved abstinence from alcohol for those who felt they could stand the strain, up to half a pint of wine was permitted each day, provided that 'excess and drunkenness do not creep in'. Even in Lent, the degree of fasting was left very much up to the individual: 'Let each one ... withdraw somewhat from food, drink and sleep.' Not excessively, not to the detriment of health, only 'somewhat'. Benedict's eating plan is a model of good sense and, apart from the provision of wine which nowadays some might consider over-generous, could have been devised by a twenty-first century dietician.

Turgot, who himself was subject to the Benedictine Rule, is revealing about Margaret's own practice in such matters. Too embarrassed in life to obey the queen's urging that he should rebuke her for her sins, after her death he could only recall his disquiet at the extent of her self-neglect. Even in periods when fasting was not required,

She hardly allowed herself the necessaries of life … her light and frugal meal excited rather than satisfied her hunger. She seemed to taste her food, rather than to take it. From this let it be considered how great her abstinence was when she fasted, when such was her abstinence when she feasted! During the forty days preceding Easter and Christmas, the abstinence with which she was in the habit of inflicting herself was incredible. So, on account of her excessive fasting, she suffered up to the end of her life from a very acute pain in the stomach.

There is plenty of evidence that even a very frugal diet did not prevent saints from living into old age. Simeon Stylites survived on top of a pillar near Antioch until he was seventy-two, Patrick died at seventy-six, Columba at seventy-five and the polymath Hildegard of Bingen at eighty-one. Even in the nineteenth century St Jean-Baptiste-Marie Vianney, the famous Curé d'Ars, sustained life until he was seventy-three on a diet said to have consisted chiefly of mouldy potatoes. Margaret's eating habits, however, seem to have transcended frugality; a lack of essential nutrients must have contributed to her debility and, finally, left her unable to fight off disease.

The question, of course, is why such a devoted Benedictine adherent should have disobeyed the Rule in this particular matter. In recent times the word 'anorexic' has been used to describe Margaret, but it is unhelpful to project the model of a contemporary psychiatric condition, most common among adolescent girls and associated with the pressures of a modern society, onto a woman who died in 1093. Margaret did not wish to be thin, nor to manipulate her family emotionally by a refusal to eat. This is not to deny, however, that she lived her life under stress, and that anxiety may have intensified her austerity as well as her fervour.

The conventional view of Margaret is of a serene, saintly figure, destined by her untroubled faith and good works for immediate entry into heaven. 'She was loosed from the chains of the flesh,' is how Florence of Worcester recorded her death, 'and passed to the joys of eternal salvation', and long before her canonisation in 1249 the words 'good' and 'saintly' were routinely prefixed to her name. This assessment, however, gives no clue to how Margaret felt about herself, of the fears and depressions against which even strongest faith is not constantly proof.

Apart from the unease which she shared with other ostentatiously wealthy people about Christ's preaching of holy poverty, and which resulted in the orgy of church endowment which so offended St Bernard, there were tensions both temporal and spiritual in Margaret's life. Her early experience was of displacement and sudden bereavement; throughout her adolescence her status was precarious, her future unpredictable and her life beset by political upheaval and danger to those she loved. Nor did marriage greatly change her situation. She may have seen in Malcolm her best hope of safety and stability, but she must also have feared for her future and that of her young family should her hot-headed husband be killed and an internecine war of succession follow – which was exactly what did happen when both she and the king were dead. She knew that life was short and unpredictable; the sudden death in 1085 of Donald, Malcolm and Ingibiorg's second son, when he was only in his early twenties, may well have caused his stepmother to shiver. It is small wonder that she liked an orderly life and sought refuge in a faith that imposed meaning on the chaos of secular life, but there were problems there too. The Christianity in which Margaret believed so fervently was not entirely consoling, for it was a religion of paradox, of love and fear, in whose teachings the hope of salvation was balanced by the certainty of judgement, not only for oneself but for one's nearest and dearest.

In a recent book, *Faith of our Fathers: Reflections on Catholic Tradition*, Professor Eamon Duffy quotes a remark that a saint, in the age of popular belief, was 'someone whose life had been insufficiently researched'. The problem with a life such as Margaret's is that a vital area of it cannot be researched at all. Margaret left no account of her inner life, but it is a reasonable guess that it was not uniformly serene. Later believers who at different periods did write of their spiritual journeys, such as the anonymous medieval author of *The Cloud of Unknowing*, St John of the Cross, St Teresa of Avila, St Thérèse of Lisieux and the twentieth-century Trappist monk Thomas Merton, all spoke of their long periods of doubt, the terrible sense of the absence of God and the temptation to despair. It seems likely that Margaret's experience was much the same. And to doubts of her own salvation and the crushing sense of unworthiness which are the dark side of Christian belief, there may have been added fears for the welfare of the souls of those closest to her.

Nothing is known of Edgar Ætheling's religious practice, but in his own time he was charged with idleness and self-indulgence, while his constant changing of allegiances suggests an opportunistic rather than a pious character. Even closer to home, Margaret of all people must have been aware of the shallowness of Malcolm's Christian conviction and, although she might take a pragmatic view of his warfaring, his casual attitude to the breaking of oaths probably worried her too. Much has been made, in defence of Malcolm, of the difference between his oaths to the Norman kings as a holder of land in England and as king in Scotland, the inference being that the latter were not morally binding. It is hard to believe that such sophistry would have cut much ice with a religious literalist like Margaret, who regarded oaths as sacred and who, as a young girl, had seen what happened to Harold Godwinsson after he broke an oath sworn to William of Normandy.

It was not only the possibility of outright hellfire that coloured the imaginations of people like Margaret. Although belief in purgatory did not become a formal church dogma until the Council of Trent in the mid-sixteenth century, the notion of an intermediate state of painful purification, which might endure for centuries before the final Judgement, had been part of Catholic teaching since the time of the 'Christian Fathers' with whose writings Margaret was so well acquainted. Remission for oneself and others could, however, be earned by faith and good works, and that is the clue to Margaret's way of life. When she prayed in a damp cave at Dunfermline or in the windy citadel at Edinburgh, spent hours reciting the Offices of the Dead, paid for Masses to be said after death for the souls of Malcolm, herself and their children, washed beggars' feet, refused to sleep and denied herself to the point of starvation, it was because she believed that her sacrifices could help to save herself and those she loved from the pains that awaited unrepentant sinners beyond the grave. If all of this seems even to modern Christians excessive, it is because they consider such an emphasis on sin and damnation morbid and, in an age of symbolism and psychological explanation, no longer interpret scripture as literally as their ancestors did. It is notable that Margaret's loss of universal popularity in Scotland has largely coincided with the twentieth-century decline in traditional Christian belief.

Although a number of English chroniclers devoted space to the death of the Anglo-Saxon granddaughter of Edmund Ironside, all their accounts rely on Turgot's, which is poignant, and rings true because he does not assign to himself a greater role than he actually had. Whether Turgot's acquaintance with the royal household was long or short, he had certainly left Dunfermline by 1087, when he was appointed prior of Durham. He does, however, preface his account of Margaret's last days with a description of a visit he paid to her shortly before, when she recounted her personal history and asked him to remember her in prayers and Masses for her soul. She expressed remorse for her sins – perhaps the vanity, haughtiness and irascibility that sometimes break the surface of an otherwise blameless life – and also, claims Turgot, begged him to care for her children.

> *When you see any of them exalted to the height of earthly dignity, go to him, warn, and when circumstances require it, censure him … lest he be puffed up with pride, or offend God with avarice, or through the prosperity of the world neglect the blessedness of life eternal.*

Probably Turgot was displaying his credentials in this passage, and there is certainly an element of being wise after the event. Although in the days before her death Margaret may well have been tormented by the vulnerability of her children, there was no certainty in 1093 that they would ever be exalted to the height of earthly dignity. Nor does it appear that subsequently Turgot was on close terms with them. Although in 1109 Alexander I was instrumental in the appointment of his mother's biographer to the bishopric of St Andrews, vacant since the death of Fothad in 1093, their relationship quickly became acrimonious and, despite Queen Matilda's having commissioned the biography, there is no evidence of any intimacy between her and Turgot. After this final, tearful visit, however, Turgot bows out of his own narrative, admitting that his account of Margaret's end is dependent on the witness of an unnamed priest. This man, whom the queen loved for his 'simplicity, innocence and purity', had become her confessor and confidant; after her death he would become a monk in the priory at Durham, and there be able to fill in the gap in Turgot's story. The clumsiness of such a literary device actually lends weight to the belief that the events recounted are broadly true.

By the spring of 1093, while Malcolm sat nursing his grievance against William Rufus, Margaret's health was declining rapidly. She was no longer able to ride and was increasingly confined to her bed. The summer must have been a difficult one and when, in August, Malcolm rode south to his conference with William Rufus, she no doubt prayed fervently for a swift and amicable resolution. Her feelings of horror and despair when Malcolm came raging home in September, stamping and shouting out his intention to teach Rufus a lesson, can easily be imagined. It speaks of her weakened condition and of the prophetic frame of mind which heralded her approaching death that, for the first time on record, Margaret begged him to change his mind.

Her pleas went unheeded. At the beginning of November, the darkest month and the worst possible time of year for a military campaign, Malcolm rode out from Edinburgh at the head of a hastily assembled army, taking with him Margaret's first and third sons, Edward and Edgar. It was Malcolm's fifth ravaging of Northumbria, but this time there was to be no return. On 13 November the Scots were ambushed on the River Aln near Alnwick Castle by Robert de Mowbray, William Rufus's recent appointee as earl, the army was put to flight and the king slain. Robert's kinsman, Arkel Morel of Bamborough, is named as the assassin, the killing a particular act of treachery since Malcolm and Morel were old friends. While his father's body was being tossed into a cart and trundled unceremoniously to Tynemouth for rough burial, Prince Edward was carried gravely wounded from the scene. He died shortly afterwards in Jed Forest, aged no more than twenty-two, leaving to Edgar the ghastly task of riding back to Edinburgh and breaking the news to the dying queen.

On the day when Malcolm met his end, Margaret was only four days away from hers and, despite anxiety about the future, probably glad of it. There was no medical treatment in the eleventh century apart from bloodletting and cauterisation, no pain relief except pagan charms and dubious herbal potions. Margaret would have been horrified by the charms and would almost certainly have spurned the potions. Her suffering was her last earthly offering to God and a Christian death, prepared for by confession and absolution, her final goal.

The priest who was Turgot's informant told him that, on the day of the king's death, the queen expressed forebodings of calamity, but then seemed to make a slight recovery. By 16 November her pain had eased sufficiently for her to rise from her bed, hear Mass and receive the holy Viaticum, the Eucharist reserved for the dying. Once back in bed, however, she was again attacked by excruciating pain and, aware that the sand of her life was trickling away, called urgently for her priests to start repeating psalms and commending her soul to Christ. She asked for her Black Cross to be brought and, after a fraught moment when the lid of its container got stuck, took it and clasped it to her. With a final spurt of energy, she lifted it heavenward while she recited the fiftieth psalm:

God, the Lord God, has spoken
And summoned the world
from the rising to the setting sun ...

Offer to God the sacrifice of thanksgiving
and pay your vows to the Most High.
If you call upon me in time of trouble,
I will come to your rescue ....

It was into this terrible scene that Edgar stumbled, dishevelled and travel-stained from his arduous journey. At the sight of him Margaret rallied enough to ask for news of Malcolm and Edward and, when the shocked and unhappy young man shrank from his task, ordered him to tell her the truth. Turgot enquires,

Who would have believed that in the midst of so many adversities she would not murmur against God? But in all these things she sinned not with her lips nor spoke foolishly against God. Rather she raised her hands and eyes to heaven and broke forth into praise and thanksgiving, saying, 'Praise and thanks I give to thee, almighty God, that thou hast been pleased that I should endure such great afflictions at my departing, and art pleased that through enduring these afflictions, I should be cleansed from some stain of sin'.

Her last words were, 'Deliver me.'

This is among the most famous deathbed scenes in Scottish history. It is based on secondhand testimony and forms the climax to a book in which fact is inextricably woven with pious exaggeration. If it rings true, it is because it sounds so consistent. Such a woman, after such a life, would have died a death like this.

II

THE LEGACY
OF MARGARET

MUCH has been made in recent times of Margaret's political role in Scotland, as if her devotion to religious life should have precluded an interest in secular affairs. She has been accused particularly of worldly ambition in encouraging Malcolm to name Edward as his chosen successor in preference to the 'Celtic' Duncan who, since being freed and knighted following the death of William the Conqueror, had been living as a Norman gentleman and displaying no inclination to return to the land of his birth. It has even been suggested that Margaret was complicit in the death of Lulach's son Mael Snechta, despite the fact that this former rebel is known to have died peacefully in his bed in a monastery, and of Malcolm and Ingibiorg's son Donald, of whom nothing is known except that he died 'unshriven' – the implication being that since he had no time to confess his sins and receive absolution, his death came suddenly and violently. There is not a shred of evidence to support such allegations, but the fact that they should even be made indicates how quickly the distressed princess of one legend can turn into the wicked stepmother of another.

It is very likely indeed that Margaret took every opportunity to promote the interest of her eldest son in the matter of the succession. It is the sort of thing mothers do. It would not be surprising either if there was an element of dynastic ambition in Margaret's urging; the son and grandson of Edmund Ironside had been pushed aside in the scramble for the throne of England, and Margaret may have seen some justice and recompense in the prospect of his great-grandson ascending another throne. Besides, she was a much younger wife who must have understood very well the position that she and her other children would be in if Malcolm, middle-aged by eleventh-century standards when they married, died and Edward did not inherit. Although she could not have known Duncan, who had been taken south as a hostage barely two years after her marriage, she had seen and heard enough of dynastic ruthlessness in her early life to know that kings do not look kindly on potential rivals. She must also have known that Duncan, who married Cospatric's daughter Æthelreda around 1090, had a young son, William, yet another male heir with a claim to the Scottish crown.

In fact, the matter was more complicated than a choice between the claims of two young princes and, when the time came, Malcolm having named Edward would only have been one point in the young man's favour. Traditionally the Scottish succession relied on a custom known as tanistry, in which what mattered in choosing a new king was descent from the kingly line, not from the last holder of the office. This meant that any male adult whose father, grandfather or great-grandfather had been king was eligible, brothers having a stronger claim than sons, and in practice allowed the strongest and ablest member of the family to be elected. This system, originating in Ireland, avoided the problems posed by a child monarch that so sorely plagued the later Stewart line, but it was bad news for the sons of Margaret, whose paternal uncle had been waiting long, bitter years for the opportunity to be king.

This man was Donald Bàn ('the Fair'), Malcolm's younger brother who, traditionally, had fled to the Norse-ruled but Gaelic-inhabited stronghold of the Western Isles when Malcolm fled to England in 1040. Now aged sixty, Donald's tastes and sympathies were entirely Gaelic; according to Hector Boece, in a passage from his sixteenth-century history of Scotland that has a strangely modern resonance, he despised 'the luxury of the soft south' and, basing his claim on the old native tradition of king-making, was bent on restoring 'the ancient virtues of the Gael'.

There is a dramatic story of how, while Margaret's body still lay in Edinburgh Castle, Donald Bàn and his army were already laying seige to the gates, so that the queen's remains had to be smuggled down the steep western crag, under cover of a 'miraculous mist' and taken away secretly to Dunfermline to be buried. That Margaret was buried at Dunfermline was true, but the rest of the story is unfortunately fanciful. Nonetheless, a large number of the nobility rallied to the Gaelic claimant who, within weeks of Malcolm's death, was elected and installed as Donald III, king of Scots at Scone. It was now that the backlash against all things Anglo-Norman was unleashed; the *Anglo-Saxon Chronicle* relates how 'all the English were driven out who before were with King Malcolm', and no doubt the decor at court was again drastically changed. The sons of Malcolm and Margaret fled to England where their uncle Edgar Ætheling, suspecting that such an influx of his relations might not be pleasing to William Rufus, made discreet arrangements for them to be billeted with friends in Normandy.

The first challenger to Donald's position was not a son of Margaret, but Ingibiorg's son Duncan, the Normanised prince who had not lived in his native land since he was twelve. It is likely that William Rufus saw in Duncan what Edward the Confessor had seen in Malcolm forty years earlier, the pleasing prospect of a grateful, compliant vassal, but, since it was he who approached the English king to ask for support for his claim, Duncan may have seen the kingship of Scotland as a just recompense for twenty years of exile. It was as 'Duncan, son of King Malcolm, by hereditary right King of Scotland' that the young man rode north with an army of English and Norman knights, his notion of inheritance as Norman as everything else about him. Interestingly, the sons of Margaret seem not to have objected to their half-brother's claim, and Edgar was one of the signatories to the charter drawn up in connection with land grants made to Durham by Duncan in 1094. By the late spring of that year the claimant was in Scotland; in May he inflicted a surprise defeat on his uncle in battle and was installed at Scone as King Duncan II.

The new king's triumph was, however, short-lived. Still in the grip of post-Margaret xenophobia, the Scots rebelled, not to depose him but to force him to rule on their terms. Since the price he had to pay for tenure was the dismissal of his entire force of English and Norman knights, Duncan was left friendless and unprotected; it comes as no surprise that in November, exactly one year after the deaths of his father and stepmother, he was murdered at Mondynes near Stonehaven by Maelpedair, the mormaer of Mearns. It is not surprising either that Donald was behind the murder, but rather more so that by now he had a new ally; Edmund, Malcolm and Margaret's eldest surviving son, had decided that his best chance for the future was to ingratiate himself with his uncle. It is all but certain that Edmund was complicit in Duncan's death and it is said that, when Donald grabbed back the throne, Edmund 'bargained for half the kingdom'. This division of spoils was an aspiration rather than an achievement, but it is likely that Edmund was granted estates in southern Scotland and named by the sonless Donald as his heir.

It is arguable that if Donald had minded his own business, he might have ruled Scotland for the rest of his life. Unfortunately and foolishly, when yet another bout of unrest broke out in England between north and south, he decided to ally himself with the rebel earl of Northumbria, Robert de Mowbray, the very man who had engineered the death of his brother. Donald's fate was sealed when de Mowbray's revolt was crushed, and the rebel earl sentenced to life imprisonment. William Rufus, determined at last to have a reliable vassal on the Scottish throne, ignored the existence of Duncan II's young son William and threw his weight behind Malcolm and Margaret's fourth son, Edgar. (The reason why the third son, Æthelred, was never considered kingly material is unknown.) It was Edgar Ætheling, soon to go on the first Crusade and destined after yet more adventures to die quietly in Huntingdonshire aged seventy, who was sent with an army to Scotland in 1097, to oust Donald Bàn and place his nephew on the throne. The *Anglo-Saxon Chronicle* records that the fighting was fierce, but inevitably Norman superiority won the day and Edgar was established as 'king and vassal to King William'. For Edgar and his brothers Alexander and David, who were to rule Scotland for the next fifty-eight years, their position as client-kings could not have been more carefully spelt out.

That it was an unchallenged arrangement is also clear. By kinship and royal marriage, particularly that of their sister Edith/Matilda to William Rufus's younger brother and successor Henry I in 1100, these kings became ever more alienated from their Gaelic roots and ever more closely integrated into the Anglo-Norman world that was their maternal inheritance. When Turgot, at Matilda's command, came to write his *Life* of Margaret, it was his subject's West Saxon ancestry that he gushed over, in particular her kinship with Edward the Confessor whose mother – unrelated by blood to Margaret – was Norman. Whether or not Margaret deliberately set out to 'Normanise' the royal house of Scotland, it was the circumstance of her sons' exile that made the process inevitable. Donald's short reign was the last roar of a dying lion; on the national and international scene, the world he represented had all but passed away.

In *The Monastic Order in England,* published in 1940, Dom David Knowles famously described Margaret's household as 'something of a nursery of saints', and it was for long accepted that her three reigning sons inherited in some unique way the Christian values and practices of the 'peace-society' learned at their mother's knee. But this view is too simplistic, and nothing points up more clearly the continuing tension between the 'peace-society' and the 'war-society', or the difficulty it presents for modern sensibility, than the treatment meted out to Donald Bàn by the pious sons of Margaret. Edmund, called by William of Malmesbury 'Margaret's only degenerate son', was condemned to life imprisonment for breaking family solidarity, but allowed to serve his time as a Cluniac monk; he died in the monastery of Montacute near Yeovil in Somerset, asking, says William, to be buried in chains, 'confessing that he suffered deservedly for the sin of fratricide'. Compared with Donald's fate, Edmund's seems a merciful one. In an act of barbarity reminiscent of the blinding of Vászoly by King Stephen in Hungary a century before, these products of the 'nursery of saints' had their elderly uncle hunted down, imprisoned, blinded and forced to do menial work, allegedly laundry. Around 1107 he was assassinated at Rescobie near Forfar on the orders of either Edgar or Alexander. No doubt his Gaelic friends ensured that the old man was honoured more in death than in life; at first he was interred at Dunkeld, but later his body was transferred to the royal burial ground of Iona. The last tanist was also the last king of Scots whose funeral rites were performed there.

The ascent of Margaret's children to kingship in Scotland and to high estate elsewhere was not accomplished without cost, but by the 1100s all that she could have wished for them, in secular and dynastic terms, had been accomplished. Despite the disastrous ending of her own and Malcolm's lives, their elder daughter was queen of England and their younger, Mary, had also made a brilliant marriage. Her husband was Eustace III, count of Boulogne, whose father had fought with the Normans at Hastings and who was directly descended from Charlemagne. Eustace and Mary's daughter, Matilda, would in turn marry Stephen of Blois, who reigned as king of England from 1135 until 1154. Very little is known of Mary, but Edith/Matilda's life is well documented. Despite her declared dislike of convent life, she emulated her mother in religious observance, enrichment of the church and charitable works, and by all accounts inherited her forceful personality.

In Scotland, the reigns of Edgar, Alexander and David were largely peaceful, which is why, recollected after the ferocious wars for independence which rocked the country in the later medieval period, they were remembered as a golden age. Perhaps the ecclesiastical achievements of Edgar and Alexander have been overstated; although Edgar gave land to the monks at Dunfermline and also at Coldingham to monks from Durham, he left the bishopric of St Andrews vacant after Fothad's death and there is no evidence of other episcopal activity in Scotland during his reign. He avoided war by making a treaty with Magnus Barelegs, the king of Norway who was causing trouble along the length of Britain's western coast; more controversially, in ceding the Hebrides to Norway he gave away Iona, the most potent symbol of the Gaelic Christian tradition to which his forefathers belonged. Edgar was said to live 'like a monk' and he was still in his early thirties when he died in 1107. He was succeeded by his younger brother, Alexander I.

If Margaret would have been pleased with the rise of her sons to what

Turgot had called 'the height of earthly dignity', she might have been less thrilled by their inability to maintain the peaceableness and respect for their seniors which she had drilled into them in the nursery. That there was no love lost between the adult brothers became clear in the reign of Alexander. Although David had remained in England throughout Edgar's reign, Edgar in his will left him a vast swathe of land south of the Forth, including Teviotdale and stretching as far west as the Solway. When Alexander, whose hatred of David was recorded by Ailred of Rievaulx, contested this malicious bequest, he fell foul of Henry I, who favoured David and threatened to intervene on his behalf. Alexander was forced to yield and David, as 'Prince of Cumbria' ruled a sizeable portion of his brother's kingdom throughout the seventeen years of his reign.

Alexander's kingship was a gift from Henry I, just as Edgar's had been from William Rufus, and he had to go on his knees and swear allegiance to get it. His ties to the English royal house were further tightened by his marriage to Sibylla, an illegitimate but acknowledged daughter of King Henry. Sibylla, unlike her predecessor as queen of Scots, was described by the gossipy William of Malmesbury as lacking 'what might have been desired of her, either in modesty of manners or in refinement of person', and the couple had no children. It is possible that the passing of the kingship from brother to brother was an arrangement intended to prevent sibling strife, yet it seems both odd and sad, considering the productiveness of their parents, that not one of the six sons of Malcolm and Margaret left a direct heir. Four died childless, Alexander's son Malcolm was illegitimate, and David's only son, Henry of Huntingdon, predeceased his father.

Alexander was perhaps no more or less pious privately than Edgar, but he was more active. He had been present at Durham when, in 1104, St Cuthbert's remains were transferred from a temporary shrine to their final resting place in the partially completed cathedral, and one of his first acts as king was to urge King Henry to appoint Turgot of Durham to the vacant see of St Andrews. This might be seen as a first step towards establishing the Benedictine ecclesiastical hegemony of which Margaret had dreamed, had he not then refused to allow Turgot, or his successor Eadmer of Canterbury, to swear obedience to English archbishops – a stubbornness of which his father would have approved.

Because of his brother David's occupation of so much of his southern kingdom Alexander, despite his strong Norman connections, was really obliged to be a 'king of Scotia'. His sphere of influence lay between the Forth and the Spey; he was busiest in the parts of the country now known as Angus and Perthshire, which held the ancient royal settlements of Abernethy and Dunkeld, and had his principal seat at Invergowrie. By some he was called 'the Strong' and 'the Fierce', and is said to have held his kingdom together 'by hard work', but he was portrayed by others as a more affable character. In his fourteenth-century *Original Chronicle of Scotland*, Andrew of Wyntoun described Alexander as delighting in visiting monasteries and enriching them with ornaments, jewels, books and vestments, and as being loving and virtuous to clerics and religious, courteous to his lieges and in judgement respectful of the law. He brought Augustinian canons from the abbey of Nostell in Yorkshire to Scone and, unlike his father but in the spirit of his mother, corresponded with the pope on matters of spiritual concern in Scotland. Perhaps due to the nobility's unwillingness to contribute financially, however, other religious foundations which Alexander proposed, and which would have helped him to drive through reform, failed to materialise. By 1124, when he joined his mother and brother in the family vault at Dunfermline, the church in Scotland was not much better integrated into the 'universal church' envisaged by Margaret than when she died thirty years before. That situation was about to change.

Although he had been ruler in his brother's southern kingdom for seventeen years, David did not become king of Scots until he was forty. He was to reign for a further twenty-nine years. Reared in England from the age of nine, David, through his sister's marriage to Henry I and his own to the heiress Maud (Matilda) de Senlis, Countess of Huntingdon, was an important figure at the English court, where he was known as 'The Queen's Brother'. Although he seems not to have introduced English settlers to his estates prior to his accession, as king he soon began to grant lands in southern Scotland to Anglo-Norman knights, most famously Robert de Brus whose descendants, through a marriage with David's great grandson, would eventually claim the throne. Of all Malcolm's sons, it was David who inherited his warlord's mentality; in the early years of his reign he was ruthless in suppressing rebellion and, in the war-torn years that followed the death of Henry I in 1135, active in support of his niece Matilda's claim to the throne of England against that of his nephew-by-marriage Stephen of Blois. Despite a disastrous defeat at the Battle of the Standard near Northallerton in Yorkshire in 1138, where most of the ten thousand dead were Scots, David escaped and by 1141 had annexed, on behalf of himself and his son, the whole of the north of England from the Ribble to the Tees.

But there was another side to David's character and, although he could have had only hazy memories of Margaret, it was he who most of all inherited her zeal for the church and who eventually fulfilled her dreams. Although, according to Ailred of Rievaulx, his was a late conversion, taking place around the time of his marriage in 1113, it was a real one. In that year he founded a Tironesian abbey at Selkirk and, three years later, wished to underscore his commitment by visiting the founding father, Bernard of Tiron, in his abbey near Chartres. He was already *en route* when news reached him that Bernard had died. As king he knew nothing of the Gaelic portion of his country, and was appalled by the secular nature of his inauguration at Scone, comparing it unfavourably with the solemn, sacramental coronations of English kings. That many of his Gaelic subjects were leery of him is shown by the substantial number who initially declared themselves for Alexander's illegitimate son Malcolm but, once he had restored peace by the sword, the new king applied himself to peaceful reform with a vigour which his mother, despite her best efforts, had failed to instil in his father.

David lavished land on the church, making a hole in the royal holdings which would rile his successors for years; it was in the seventeenth century that James VI & I sarcastically called him 'ane sair sanct for the croune'. David created the diocesan system that had eluded Lanfranc. He strengthened still further ties with Durham, brought Augustinian and Tironesian monks to Kelso, Inchcolm and his own foundation of Holyrood, and built the tiny oratory in Edinburgh Castle in memory of his mother. At Dunfermline he levelled the church she had built and replaced it with a great Romanesque church and royal sepulchre, the nave of which can still be seen today. By this act he provided a magnificent location for the cult of St Margaret, which thrived after her canonisation in 1249. In David, warlord and Christian king, the salient traits of both his parents were united. There is no more striking example of how the values of the 'war-society' and the 'peace-society' accommodated each other in the medieval world.

12

THE MAKING
OF A SAINT

IF Queen Margaret had died at the end of the twentieth century, she would have been extravagantly mourned but, without a structure of institutional reverence to support her, would have faded quickly from the public consciousness. Instead, she died at the end of the eleventh, when the church provided structure, personal faith was the only coping strategy in a life of poverty, disease and early death, and the intercession of those who had lived holy lives was universally believed to ease the difficult path to heaven. She also died on the cusp of the great age of pilgrimage, when a craze for wonder working and faith healing gripped the imagination of a populace without a vestige of scientific understanding. Shrines became the destinations of rich and poor, whose frame of mind oddly combined religious fervour and holiday spirit, and relics of the saints were eagerly acquired and proudly displayed. The most successful shrines were those which recorded the largest numbers of miracles, and there developed a great appetite for stories of the saints and amazing deeds allegedly performed through their mediation. It was to the mindset of this world, both devout and credulous, that Margaret owed her posthumous celebrity.

Long before Turgot's *Life of St Margaret*, other saints' lives had been written. In a flurry of Irish monastic hagiography in the seventh century, the careers of many minor saints had been piously recorded alongside those of the three great patrons of Ireland, Patrick, Brigid and Columba. These works, of which Muirchú's *Life of St Patrick*, Tirechán's *Account of St Patrick's Journey* and Adomnán's *Life of St Columba* are probably best known today, have much in common. All were the work of clerics and, although they have a thin factual thread, their writers were less concerned with life events than in talking up their subjects' importance by recounting their miracles. To a modern reader the books appear fantastical, and have the unfortunate effect of presenting the saints as amoral and sometimes casually malign magicians, uncomfortably like the 'druids' whose teachings they sought to overthrow. Compared with these lurid and at best folkloric accounts, Turgot's work does seem downbeat and sincere, which is why it was still accepted at face value long after other saints' lives had been dismissed as products of primitive imaginations.

Apart from the incident at St Laurence's church, in which the queen so dramatically came off second best, Turgot offers his reader only one miracle. He tells how a richly ornamented Gospel book belonging to Margaret was being carried by one of her retainers who, while crossing a ford, carelessly dropped it in the water. When the loss was discovered a search was launched and, after some time, the book was located and fished out again. Despite its pages having been constantly ruffled by the current, the paper was white and the inky letters unblurred – indeed, apart from the loss of some little pieces of silk and a slight dampening of the end leaves, the book was intact, and Turgot is in no doubt that 'this miracle was wrought by our Lord because of his love for this venerable queen'. In fact, it was quite a familiar type of miracle. Adomnán records that a book copied by 'the holy hand of Columba' lay for twenty days in the River Boyne before emerging unscathed, while a hymnal penned by him lay in another river for six months. A similar marvel involved a copy of the Lindisfarne Gospels, and it would be possible to dismiss Turgot's miracle as merely a literary imitation – except that its aftermath is at least as astonishing as the miracle itself.

As recently as 1877, an illustrated and gold-embellished manuscript book of thirty-eight pages, containing extracts from the four Gospels, was bought by the Bodleian Library in Oxford from a Bristol bookseller named William Brice. Described as 'a little octavo volume of manuscript in a shabby brown binding', and originally thought to be of fourteenth-century provenance, it had previously been in a small parish library at Brent Ely in Suffolk. Experts who examined it at the Bodleian agreed that the writing was in fact eleventh-century, and were further intrigued by a poem, in Latin, inscribed on the flyleaf, mentioning that the book had once belonged to a king and a holy queen, and giving an exact account of the miracle described by Turgot. More intriguingly still, the end papers were shrunk in a way consistent with their having once been in contact with water. It is assumed that the book was buried with Margaret and stolen when her tomb was ransacked at the Reformation, but what happened to the jewelled binding and how the pages survived for eight hundred years will never be known. But it is now generally accepted that the manuscript, which the Bodleian Library acquired for six pounds and which remains a treasure in its collection, was indeed 'St Margaret's Gospel Book'.

It used to be believed that Turgot's *Life of St Margaret* represented a watershed in the development of writing about saints, that by the eleventh century the church had matured beyond the point of requiring to validate itself by making preposterous claims on behalf of its holy people. In fact, it was a one-off. Well into the twelfth century works in the earlier genre were still being produced; the *Life of St Ninian* by Ailred of Rievaulx and the *Life of St Kentigern* by Jocelin of Furness stretch credulity no less than Adomnán's *Life of St Columba*. Although it was well known that very soon after her death Margaret became an informal 'cult figure', the absence of other written evidence led to the assumption that Turgot's rather tame miracle was the only one on record concerning her. It was also thought that, at the time of her official canonisation, there might have been some difficulty in scraping together the required evidence of miraculous events. That this perception was wide of the mark has only recently come to light.

In 2003 a book was published with the title *The Miracles of St Æbba of Coldingham and St Margaret of Scotland*. It was edited by Professor Robert Bartlett of the University of St Andrews, who provided an English translation alongside the original Latin. The manuscript, which dates from the reign of King James III (1460-88) and contains matter relating to other saints besides Æbbe and Margaret, was discovered by Professor Bartlett in the Biblioteca del Palacio Real in Madrid; the 'Margaret' material comprises a variant version of Turgot's *Life* plus a collection of forty miracles said to have been witnessed at her shrine. Almost all are of healing, of afflictions ranging from blindness and cancer to demon possession and a stomach full of lizards. The section relating to miracles is a copy of the original composed in the thirteenth century and probably prepared as evidence for Margaret's claim to canonisation. It is almost certainly from the *scriptorium* of the abbey at Dunfermline, and is known to have been taken to Spain, where there was a special interest in Scottish saints, by the Count of Gondomar, Spanish ambassador to the court of James VI & I in the early seventeenth century. It was acquired by the Biblioteca del Palacio Real in 1807, and lay there unregarded for close on two hundred years before being noticed by Professor Bartlett when he was actually looking for something else.

The strange posthumous life of Margaret began not long after her death, when her grave, conveniently situated on the pilgrim route through Fife to St Andrews, itself became a place of pilgrimage. It is unsurprising that the poor people of Dunfermline, bereft of her patronage and with no medical help for their numerous afflictions, came to pray in the church where she was buried, or that, in the fervid religious atmosphere of the time, rumours of cures and prayers answered began to spread. The queen who had borne eight children acquired a reputation for helping pregnant women, and the allegedly miraculous power of her undergarment led to its being carefully preserved. Both Margaret Tudor, wife of James IV (1488-1513) and Mary of Guise, wife of James V (1513-42) paid the monks at Dunfermline for the loan of 'Queen Margaret's sark' when they went into labour, and as late as 1566 Mary, queen of Scots had it brought to Edinburgh Castle for the birth of her son.

Soon word of the late queen's intercessory power was carried far beyond Dunfermline. Crowds of the sick and the pious and the curious thronged to her shrine, rich mingling with poor, as they were doing to shrines all over Scotland and England in the belief that pilgrimage brought remission from purgatory and helped to cancel out sin. As elsewhere, lights and sparks were seen around the grave and miraculous cures claimed. When in 1199 Margaret's great-grandson King William 'the Lion' (1156-1214) spent a night beside her tomb, and was warned 'by a divine oracle not to invade England with an army', he was so overawed that he publicly asserted her sainthood – so giving a royal endorsement of what was already commonly held to be true.

Meanwhile, the building and adapting of the church for its new role as a pilgrimage centre went on apace. Around 1123 a body, identified as Malcolm III's solely by the great length of its bones, was exhumed at Tynemouth and brought back to Dunfermline by Alexander I, who buried it beside Margaret's in front of the high altar. In 1150, when David I's great work of reconstruction was nearing completion, Margaret's remains were elevated into a stone tomb directly above her original resting-place, the first of many disturbances of her bones. In the early thirteenth century, with canonisation in the offing, the east end of the abbey was again remodelled, this time to relocate the high altar and provide an 'ambulatory route' through which pilgrims filed to reach a new chapel designed to house the relics of the saint.

In 1246 Margaret's great great-grandson, Alexander II (1198-1249) petitioned Pope Innocent IV that Margaret, Queen of Scots, be officially instated in the Catalogue of Saints. As usual on these occasions, inquiries were ordered into the queen's life and miracles, now known to have been more numerous and better documented than previously realised. The pope warned that no 'undue haste' was possible, yet only three years later he issued a decree that the canonisation of 'Margaret, Queen of Scots, of blessed memory' should proceed forthwith. It has been suggested that the abbot of Dunfermline lent his weight to the request because the abbey desperately needed the income generated by pilgrims for the upkeep of the now extensive buildings, and certainly, by this time, commercial considerations were an important aspect of any shrine's functioning. But the acceleration of the process was mainly a reward for Scots participation in the Crusades, the 'wars of the Cross' then being waged against Muslims for control of the holy sites in Palestine. In 1247 one-twentieth of all church revenues in the diocese of Dunkeld were set aside for this purpose, and the following year the bishops of Glasgow and St Andrews were made collectors of all money intended to support the current Crusade.

So it was that on 19 June 1250, in the presence of her great great great-grandson, the eight year-old Alexander III, and a vast throng of nobility, bishops, clerics, and pilgrims, Margaret's tomb was opened. As the sweet per-fume then believed to be the odour of sanctity but now recognised as the smell of enbalming fluid scented the air, the bones were lifted and transferred to an ornately gilded reliquary called a *chasse*, which was then carried in procession to the high altar. (There is some disagreement about when exactly the head was detached from the rest of the body, but it likely to have been at this time; it was subsequently displayed separately in a head-shaped case with a crystal at the base of the neck, through which pilgrims could see locks of the queen's 'auburn' hair.) In a moment of high drama, it was reported that as the *chasse* was borne past Malcolm's adjacent grave, it suddenly became so heavy that no degree of effort could shift it – a problem only solved when a voice was heard declaring that it was against the saint's wishes to be separated from her husband. It was decided to allow Malcolm's remains to lie next to those of his wife, a proximity that accorded him in death rather more of a saintly reputation than he had ever earned in life.

The final destination of the *chasse* was the new chapel, where it was placed on a pillared pedestal of white-flecked Frosterly marble, the 'sacred stone' quarried in County Durham and used principally for fonts, altar steps and tombs. Most of the time the *chasse* was concealed by a wooden cover, but on the saint's feast days (19 June and 16 November) this was lifted to give pilgrims closer access; they were allowed to take pinches of 'sacred dust' and push small votive offerings between the pillars. By papal decree, forty days of remission from purgatory were earned by those who made a pilgrimage to St Margaret's shrine. The *chasse* and the pillars that supported it have long since disap-peared, but the pedestal can still be seen outside the abbey church in Dunfermline – the only fragment of the shrine to survive the iconoclasm of later years.

The veneration of relics – the bones, ashes, garments and other possessions of holy persons – has a long history, and not only a Christian one, although it has been an important aspect of both Roman Catholic and Orthodox worship since very early times. Queen Margaret herself venerated the relics of St Andrew, said to have included a kneecap and some fingers. In its purest form, such devotion is a show of reverence for the earthly remains of martyrs and those believed to have had a special relationship with God, 'in order,' explained St Jerome in the fourth century, 'the better to adore him whose martyrs they are'. The notion that relics in themselves have magical and curative powers has always been strenuously denied by the church, and cures associated with them ascribed entirely to the will of God. Early writers, including those studied by Margaret, stressed that the bones of saints must always be shown the greatest respect; the unwrapping and touching of the body of a martyr was regarded by them as a perilous enterprise, to be performed by only the holiest ecclesiastics after much fasting and prayer. It is clear from many sources that our remote ancestors, whether Christian or not, would have found incomprehensible our belief that ideally remains should not be disturbed at all.

No matter how reverent the early Christians were, however, by the great age of pilgrimage in the twelfth and thirteenth centuries the purity of their practice and intention had been sullied. The enrichment of the church had led to corruption and, while a visit to a shrine remained a valid spiritual experience for many individuals, pilgrimage generally had got out of hand. The desire to enhance the status of their own shrines led to compulsive relic-gathering by cathedrals, monasteries and even parish churches; bitter rivalries surfaced between different shrines, corpses were tastelessly dismembered and body parts passed around. Worse still, false relics multiplied – teeth, fingers, drops of blood, shreds of shrouds and fragments of the Cross were cynically peddled by the unscrupulous and mercenary to the desperate and credulous. Not until the Council of Trent, convened in 1545 with the dual aims of countering Protestantism and removing the abuses which had defaced the church's reputation, were these excesses reined in with the insistence that 'in the invocation of saints, the veneration of relics and the sacred use of images, every superstition shall be removed and all filthy lucre abolished'. But it was too late to prevent the Reformation, which in Scotland had dire consequences for the shrine of St Margaret.

It has been said that the Reformation came to Dunfermline on 28 March 1560, when the abbey was attacked by a Protestant mob. The choir and sanctuary of the church were destroyed, the royal tombs and St Margaret's shrine vandalised. It seems, however, that the monks, who had for some time been threatened and abused in the streets, had seen how the wind was blowing, and before the attack had secretly removed the contents of Margaret's reliquary for safe keeping. The bones were taken to nearby Craigluscar, where the abbot, George Durie, had a private estate. There they lay hidden until 1580 when, according to the life of Margaret in the *Acta Sanctorum*, the great hagiographical dictionary published in Antwerp by the followers of the Flemish Jesuit Jean Bolland (1596-1665):

> ... *Catholicism in Scotland being then finally despaired of,* [King] *Philip* [of Spain] *made it his business to cause the relics of the sainted sovereigns to be searched for and brought to his new church.*

This was at the monastery of St Laurence at the Escorial, outside Madrid. There the bones were encased in a new shrine, King Philip having 'obtained relief delineations to be preserved, with the aid of the chisel, for posterity'. This squares with the description of the writer Sir George MacKenzie (1636-91) of 'one repository, with their images on the outside and this inscription, "Malcolm, King and St Margaret, Queen"'. The shrine was dedicated in 1586, and was still to be seen at the end of the eighteenth century.

The head of Queen Margaret, as we know, fared differently. To amplify: it was first taken to Edinburgh Castle on the orders of Mary, queen of Scots, who seemed determined to surround herself with relics of her fruitful predecessor as she awaited the birth of her own child. After she fled to England in 1567, the head was placed in the care of a Benedictine monk and taken back to Craigluscar, where it remained for thirty years before being smuggled to Antwerp by a Jesuit priest named John Robie. A further twenty-three years passed before Bishop John Malderus authenticated it and licensed it as an object of veneration, and seven more before it made its last known journey to the Scots College at Douai. In 1785 it was witnessed by James Carruthers. During the violently anti-clerical French Revolution, which began in 1789, the college was destroyed and the head disappeared.

There is a touching postscript to this sad story. The despair felt in 1580 for the future of the Catholic church in Scotland was natural but premature; the faith was kept quietly alive, mostly in the Highlands, through the religious strife of the seventeenth century and the Jacobite unrest of the eighteenth, until in the nineteenth it was strengthened by an influx of mainly Irish and

Italian immigrants. In 1827 there arrived in Edinburgh a young priest named James Gillis (1802-64) who had been born and educated in Canada, the son of a Banffshire emigré father and a Canadian mother. A charismatic, energetic preacher and pastor who made many converts, James Gillis was equally popular among rich and poor. He was a tireless fundraiser for many projects, but the one closest to his heart was the foundation of a convent, which would be the first in Scotland since the Reformation. By 1831 his powers of persuasion and command of French had raised the necessary money in France, and the Ursuline convent, dedicated to St Margaret, was opened in 1835.

In 1852, James Gillis succeeded Bishop Andrew Carruthers (the younger brother of the historian who saw the head of Queen Margaret in 1785) as Vicar Apostolic of the Eastern District of Scotland. He had heard of the existence of relics of St Margaret in Madrid and, with the thirtieth anniversary of the opening of the convent pending, he decided to approach the Spanish government, through Pope Pius IX, in the hope of having them returned to Edinburgh and laid in the convent chapel. He was also keen to acquire two portraits, one of Malcolm and one of Margaret, known to be in the Escorial. Permission for the transfer of the relics was given in principle but, with the Spanish authorities prevaricating, Bishop Gillis decided to go to Madrid in person and arrange for their transfer to Edinburgh. The bishop was not only an enthusiastic priest, he was also a born writer and, in an unpublished document in the possession of the Scottish Catholic Archives, he describes vividly the sheer frustration of his quest.

Arriving in Spain after a long overland journey, the first disaster to overtake him was the loss of his portmanteau. As he spent nine sweltering days trying to locate St Margaret's relics, the reason for the authorities' equivocating became all too clear; the shrine was gone and almost all of its contents 'mislaid'. At this point the official detailed to assist was taken ill with a raging fever. To give him time to recover, Bishop Gillis went off to visit the *curé* of the French church, only to discover that he had gone to Bayonne for a couple of months. One good piece of news was that the lost portmanteau had been found, but unfortunately by the time the bishop returned to his hotel to collect it, it had been lost again. He went to the Escorial without it but, despite having a written decree from the king, still failed to persuade the curator to hand over the one meagre relic that had actually been found.

By this time Bishop Gillis was weary and longing to get home, but his troubles were not yet over. On Saturday he went to confession, but the priest had gone out. He managed to contact the queen, who said he could have the relic, but there were further petty official objections to his taking it without formal permission also from the king. This took several days to arrive, and related only to the relic. The request for the portraits of Malcolm and Margaret was refused, and in the end all Bishop Gillis had to bring back to Edinburgh was one piece of bone, about fifteen centimetres long. The last, exhausted words of his account were, 'Oh, Spain!' The fragment, thought to be from a shoulder, was however lovingly and reverently received. Labelled *de Sancta Margarita*, it was placed in a neo-Gothic monstrance, and is treasured in the Edinburgh convent of the Ursulines to this day.

If the Victorian Bishop Gillis's adventures in Spain seem but tenuously connected to the distant, archaic Scotland where Margaret spent half her life, they seem little closer to Scotland only a century and a half later, where the *Zeitgeist* is edgier, more critical and much less devout. Anti-English sentiment, which has its roots in the battle for independence in the fourteenth century, has for some Scots coloured their view of eleventh-century Margaret, and as a nation we are perhaps less inclined to take virtue at face value. Yet the fact remains that, for almost a thousand years, Margaret had a strong grip on the imagination of Scots of all denominations. This was due to the power of a story in which truth, faith and fantasy combined to create the myth that inspired art and writing, the naming of wells and stones, the dedication of churches, institutions and schools. If that grip has weakened, it is because many modern Scots prefer a different kind of story; Margaret's elevated status, uncompromising beliefs and rigid morality are not fashionable, and modern celebrities represent quite different aspirations and dreams. Her influence has been reappraised; we are less ready to believe that she reformed our church and rearranged our state, or that she did more than initiate the 'Normanised' Scotland that was in place seventy years after she died. So is there anything left of enduring appeal?

One answer is that, even if her achievements have been over-inflated, her personal generosity and commitment to the relief of suffering have not, and it is this aspect of her life that can still speak eloquently to an age perplexed by similar distress on a global scale. Of course Margaret was not alone among kings and queens of her time in her work of charity; the much-maligned Macbeth and Cnut gave alms liberally, while Edward the Confessor, William the Conqueror and their wives all endowed abbeys, one of whose important functions was poor relief. In the reign of Henry III (1216-72) upwards of two thousand poor people were fed in one day in Westminster Great Hall, and the distribution of 'the royal Maundy' to the poor on the day before Good Friday still exists in a ceremonial form. What made Margaret heroic were her awesome energy and commitment, and her fearless, hands-on approach; for her throwing money at the problem of poverty was simply not enough. As well as pressing coins into outstretched hands, she provided meals and helped to serve them, went down on her knees to wash sore, dirty feet, fed orphans with her own spoons and 'persuaded' her courtiers to give the clothes off their backs to beggars in the street.

Although the story of Margaret's paying the ransoms of English slaves brought back by Malcolm from Northumbria is, for political reasons, unlikely to be true, it speaks of a reputation for compassion, as does the faintly comic tale of hordes of beggars from England and abroad descending on Scotland, to the indignation of the native mendicants, as word of the queen's liberality spread. Certainly the nationality of her petitioners would not have mattered to Margaret. All she saw was their need, and her responsibility to alleviate it. It is sentimental to suppose that she felt personal affection for the wretched paupers she aided for the love of Christ but, at a time when poverty meant filth, stench and contagious disease and the rich generally recoiled in revulsion from the poor, her refusal to be scared or disgusted is admirable.

There is a lovely story embedded in Turgot's narrative:

On Maundy Thursday, and at High Mass, [the King] *used to make an offering of gold coins, and some of these* [Margaret] *would often piously steal and give away to the beggar who was importuning her for alms. Often indeed the King, who was quite aware of what she was doing though he pretended not to know anything about it, was greatly amused at this kind of theft, and sometimes, when he caught her in the act with the coins in her hand, would jocularly threaten to have her arrested, tried and condemned.*

It is warm, human vignettes like this and the one of Margaret having special baby-food prepared and feeding tiny children on her lap with her own spoons, that make her a much more appealing person than the fine lady of legend, with her mission to improve our manners, interfere with our church and put the stamp of Englishness upon our nation.

BIBLIOGRAPHY

(a) BOOKS

ADOMNÀN, *Life of St Columba*, ed. A. O. and M. O. Anderson (Oxford 1991).

ANDERSON, A. O., *Scottish Annals from English Chronicles 500-1265* (London 1908).

ANDERSON, A. O., *Early Sources of Scottish History*, vol. 2 (Edinburgh 1922).

Anglo-Saxon Chronicle, trans. and ed. G. N. Garmonsway (London 1990).

BAKER, D., 'A Nursery of Saints: St Margaret of Scotland Revisited' in *Medieval Women*, ed. D. Baker (Oxford 1978).

BARLOW, F., *The English Church 1000-1066* (London 1979).

——————, *Edward the Confessor* (London 1997).

——————, *The Feudal Kingdom of England 1042-1216* (London 1999).

——————, trans. and ed. *The Life of King Edward who Rests at Westminster* (Oxford 1992).

——————, *The Godwins* (London 2002).

BARROW, G. W. S., *Kingship and Unity: Scotland 1000-1306*, 2nd edition (Edinburgh 2003).

——————, *The Kingdom of the Scots* (London 1973).

——————, *Feudal Britain* (London 1956).

——————, 'The Companions of the Ætheling' in *Anglo-Norman Studies* XXV, ed. J. Gillingham (Woodbridge 2003).

BARTLETT R., trans. and ed., *The Miracles of St Æbba of Coldingham and St Margaret of Scotland* (Oxford 2003).

BARNETT, T. RATCLIFFE, *Margaret of Scotland: Queen and Saint* (Edinburgh 1926).

BATESON, D., *Scottish Coins* (Princes Risborough 1987).

BEDE (trans L. Sherley-Price), *A History of the English Church and People* (Harmondsworth 1955).

BISHOP, M., *The Pelican Book of the Middle Ages* (Harmondsworth 1983).

BRIDGEFORD, A., *1066: The Hidden History of the Bayeux Tapestry* (London 2004).

BURLEIGH, J. H. S., *A Church History of Scotland* (London 1960).

The Cambridge Biographical Encyclopaedia, ed. D. Crystal, 2nd edition (Cambridge 1998).

COULTON, G. G., *Scottish Abbeys and Social Life* (Cambridge 1933).

CUNNINGHAM, J., *The Church History of Scotland* (Edinburgh 1882).

DAWSON, C., ed. G. J. Russello, *Christianity and European Culture* (Washington DC 1998).

——————, *The Making of Europe* (New York 1956).

DICKINSON, W. CROFT and DUNCAN, A. A. M., *Scotland from Earliest Times to 1603*, 3rd edition (Oxford 1977).

DICKSON, C. and J., *Plants and People in Ancient Scotland* (Stroud 2000).

Domesday Book, trans. and ed. A. Williams and G. H. Martin (London 2002).

DONALDSON, G., *Scotland: Church and Nation through Sixteen Centuries* (London 1960).

——————, *Scottish Church History* (Edinburgh 1985).

DRISCOLL, S., *Alba: The Gaelic Kingdom of Scotland* (Edinburgh 2002).

DUFFY, E., *Faith of our Fathers: Reflections on Catholic Tradition* (London 2004).

DUNBAR, A. H., *Scottish Kings: A Revised Chronology of Scottish History 1005-1625* (Edinburgh 1899).

DUNCAN, A. A. M., *Scotland: The Making of the Kingdom* (Edinburgh 1975).

——————, *The Kingship of the Scots 842-1292* (Edinburgh 2002).

DUNLOP, E. and KAMM, A., *Kings and Queens of Scotland* (Glasgow 1984).

FINUCANE, R. C., *Miracles and Pilgrims* (London 1977).

HENDERSON, E., *The Annals of Dunfermline 1069-1878* (Glasgow 1879).

HUNNEYCUTT, L. L., *Matilda of Scotland: A Study in Medieval Queenship* (Woodbridge 2003).

JOHNSON, L. R., *Central Europe: Enemies, Neighbors, Friends* (New York 2002).

KAPELLE, W. E., *The Norman Conquest of the North* (Chapel Hill NC 1979).

KOENIGSBERGER, H. G., *Medieval Europe 400-1500* (New York 1987).

KNOWLES, D., *The Monastic Order in England* (Cambridge 1940).

LACEY, R. and DANZIGER D., *The Year 1000* (London 1999).

LAPIDGE, M., BLAIR, J., KEYNES, S. and SCRAGG, D., *The Blackwell Encyclopaedia of Anglo-Saxon England* (Oxford 1999).

LEFF, G., *Medieval Thought: St Augustine to Ockham* (Harmondsworth 1958).

LEYSER, H., *Medieval Women: A Social History of Women in England 450-1500* (London 1995).

LOYN, H. R., *The English Church 940-1154* (Harlow 2000).

LUSCOMBE, D., *Medieval Thought* (Oxford 1997).

LYNCH, M., *Scotland: A New History* (London 1991).

MacEWEN, A. C., *A History of the Church in Scotland (to 1560)* (London 1913).

McDONALD, R. A., *Outlaws of Medieval Scotland: Challenges to the Canmore Kings 1058-1266* (Phantassie, East Linton 2003).

MacQUARRIE, A., *The Saints of Scotland: Essays in Church History 450-1093* (Edinburgh 1997).

MARSHALL, R. K., *Scottish Queens 1034-1714* (Phantassie, East Linton 2003).

MENZIES, L., *Saint Margaret Queen of Scotland* (London 1935).

MUMFORD, L., *The City in History* (London 1961).

NAGY, K., *St Margaret of Scotland and Hungary* (Glasgow 1973).

The New English Bible with Apocrypha (Oxford & Cambridge 1970).

ORAM, R., *The Canmores: Kings and Queens of the Scots 1040-1290* (Stroud 2002).

REYNOLDS, A., *Later Anglo-Saxon England: Life and Landscape* (Stroud 1999).

RICHARDS, J. D., *Viking Age England* (London 1991).

RITCHIE, R. L. G., *The Normans in Scotland* (Edinburgh 1954).

SINCLAIR, W., *St Margaret, Queen of Scotland: Her Family History and Links with Europe* (Dunfermline 1993).

SKENE, W. F., *Celtic Scotland: A History of Ancient Alban*, 3 volumes (Edinburgh 1886-1890).

SORRELL, A., ed. Sorrell, M., *Reconstructing the Past* (London 1981).

STEANE, J. M., *The Archaeology of Power: England and Northern Europe 800-1600* (Stroud 2001).

STENTON, F., *Anglo-Saxon England*, 3rd edition (Oxford 1971).

TURGOT, trans. W. M. Metcalfe, 'The Life of Saint Margaret' in *Lives of the Scottish Saints* (Paisley 1895).

WILLIAM (of MALMESBURY), ed. Maynors, R. A. B., Thomson, R. M. and Winterbottom, M., *Gesta Regum Anglorum: The History of the English Kings* (Oxford 1998-99).

WILSON, A. J., *St Margaret: Queen of Scotland*, 2nd edition (Edinburgh 2001).

YEOMAN, P., *Pilgrimage in Medieval Scotland* (London 1999).

(b) ONLINE SOURCES

The Catholic Encyclopaedia
  www.newadvent.org/cathen

The Holy Rule of St Benedict trans. Rev. B. Verheyen, OSB
  www.ccel.org/b/benedict/rule2/rule.html

Matrix Monasticon
  monasticmatrix.usc.edu/monasticon

The Oxford Dictionary of National Biography 2004
  www.oxforddnb.com/view/printable/17859

(c) ARTICLES AND PAPERS

AITCHESON, G., 'King Malcolm III and Queen Margaret' (Dunfermline Abbey 2000).

GILLIS, J., unpublished papers of Bishop James Gillis 1802-1864 (Scottish Catholic Archives, Edinburgh).

PATERSON, B., 'Margaret – Saint and Politician?' (History Scotland 2004).

McROBERTS, D., 'St Margaret, Queen of Scotland' (Catholic Truth Society 1957).

ROBERTSON, G., 'Queen Margaret – How important was she to Scotland?' (Inverkeithing Local History Society Journal 2004).

PLACES TO VISIT

Abbot House Heritage Centre, Dunfermline
tel. 01383 733266
www.abbothouse.co.uk

15th-century house with a video and series of tableaux recreating the history of the house, the abbey and the town. Contains a reinterpretation of the lost head shrine of St Margaret by Walter Awlson D.A.

Dunfermline Abbey and Palace
tel. 01381 739026
www.dunfermlineabbey.co.uk

The base of St Margaret's shrine can be seen outside the east gable. The foundations of her church are under the nave built by David I, dedicated in 1147 and considered the finest Norman architecture in Scotland. The parish church of 1818, built on the site of the 12th-century choir, has a stained glass window commemorating King Robert the Bruce (1306-1329) and one commemorating King Malcolm and Queen Margaret, with their marriage as its main focus. The coat of arms of Queen Margaret and armorial banners are on display.

The ruins of the 15th-century Royal Palace are reached through a gatehouse containing carved stones from the abbey buildings.

St Margaret's Cave, Dunfermline
tel. 01383 314228

Queen Margaret is believed to have used the cave as a place of meditation and prayer. Adjacent to the Glen Bridge car park, it is accessed by a tunnel and eighty-seven descending steps. The cave contains a statue and there are explanatory displays.

St Margaret's Stone

The stone is half a mile west of Pitreavie, half way between North Queensferry and Dunfermline. It is said to mark a favoured resting place of Margaret on journeys to and from Dunfermline; traditionally she received petitions and dispensed advice here. The stone was subsequently visited by women anxious to conceive, or hoping for a trouble-free birth.

**St Margaret's Chapel,
Edinburgh Castle**

tel. 0131 225 9846
www.historic-scotland.gov.uk

The chapel is the oldest building in
Edinburgh, dating from the 1120s.
It had a fine Norman-style chancel
arch and stained glass by Douglas
Strachan, presented when the
chapel was restored in 1934. There
is a copy of St Margaret's Gospel
book, and ten bench seats with
roundels carved with symbols of
St Margaret.

**St Margaret's Well,
Edinburgh**

Situated in Holyrood Park, opposite
the Palace of Holyrood House, the
vaulted well house dates from the
15th century and was moved to this
site from Meadowbank in 1860.
The well is fed by a natural spring.

INDEX

Acta Sanctorum 95

Adalbert (St), bishop of Prague 17, 18

Adelhaid, wife of Prince Géza 16, 17

Adomnán, abbot of Iona 62, 89, 90, 91

Æbbe, St 91

Ælfwine, bishop of Romsey 22

Ælgifu, mother of Harold Harefoot 20

Æthelred II, the Unready, king of the English 8-9, 20, 24

Æthelred, son of Margaret 50, 51, 58, 84

Æthelreda, daughter of Cospatric 82

Æthelstan, son of Æthelred II 9

Agatha, mother of Margaret 12-13, 14, 18, 19, 22, 23, 24, 25, 34-5, 36, 38, 39, 53, 65

Agnes of Poitou, mother of Henry IV 22

Aidan, (St), abbot of Lindisfarne 57

Ailred of Rievaulx 24-5, 36, 67, 86, 88, 91

Alan the Red, count of Richmond 70

Aldwin, monk of Jarrow 6, 63

Alexander I, king of Scots 50, 51-2, 78, 84-7, 88, 92

Alexander II, king of Scots 92

Alexander III, king of Scots 93

Alexander II, Pope 50

Alfred, son of Æthelred II 20

Anastasia, daughter of Prince Jaraslow 12

Andrew I, king of Hungary 12, 13, 14, 15, 16, 18, 19, 22, 24, 50

Andrew of Wyntoun 87

Andrew, St 65, 94

Anglo-Saxon Chronicle 4, 9, 24, 33, 43, 65-6, 67, 68, 70, 82, 84

Anund Jakob, prince of Sweden 11

Árpád, Magyar chief 16

Astrid, wife of Olaf II of Norway 11

Augustine, (St), of Canterbury 58, 73

Augustine, St, of Hippo 28

Baldwin, count of Flanders 32

Barrow, Professor G. W. S. 11

Bartlett, Professor Robert 91

Bede, Venerable 57

Benedict, St 27, 28-9, 55, 56-7, 72, 74

Bernard, St, of Clairvaux 49, 76

Bernard, (St), abbot of Tiron 88

Bertin, Goscelin de, monk 73

Blackadder, Robert 2

Bolland, Jean, Jesuit priest and scholar 95

Bower, Walter 3

Brice, William, bookseller 90

Brigid, St 89

Bruce, Robert, great-grandson of David I 87

Brudei, king of the Picts 57

Bruno, Bishop 16

Bruno, count of Brunswick 12-13, 58

Brus, Robert de 87

Carruthers, Bishop Andrew
96
Carruthers, James 1, 95, 96
Cassian 28
Causley, Charles 3
Cerdic, king of Wessex 8
Charlemagne, king and
emperor 85
Charles II, king of England
and Scotland 48
Christina, sister of Margaret
14, 22, 26, 28, 34-5, 36,
38, 39, 53, 65, 66, 72
Cloud of Unknowing, The
76
Cnut, king of England and
Denmark 5, 9, 10-11, 12,
19, 20, 21, 25, 97
Colman, monk of Iona 58
Columba, St 40, 41, 45, 57,
62, 75, 89, 90
Comines, Robert de,
earl of Northumbria 38
Conrad II, emperor
of Germany 13
Conrad III, king of
Burgundy 13
Constantine the Great 60-1
Cospatric, earl of
Northumbria 35, 36, 38,
70, 82
Crinan, abbot of Dunkeld
42, 58
Cuthbert, St 25, 57-8, 69,
71, 86

David I, king of Scots 24,
25, 50, 51-2, 74, 84, 85-6,
87-8, 92
Dawson, Christopher 17

Dolfin, ruler in Carlisle 70
Domesday Book 66
Donald, son of Malcolm III
42, 76, 81
Donald Bàn, brother of
Malcolm III 41, 82-5
Douay Chronicle 48, 65
Duffy, Professor Eamon
76
Duncan I, king of Scots
41, 53
Duncan II, king of Scots
52-3, 81-2, 83, 84
Duncan, son of Malcolm III
42
Duncan, Professor A. A. M.
44, 63
Dunfermline, abbot of
(1246) 92-3
Durie, George, abbot of
Dunfermline 95

Eadmer, bishop of
St Andrews 86
Eadric Streona, son-in-law
of Æthelred II 9, 10
Ealdgyth, grandmother of
Margaret 9, 10, 11
Ealdred, bishop of
Worcester, archbishop of
York 21, 22, 34
Edgar I, king of Scots
50, 51-2, 79, 80, 83, 84-6,
87
Edgar I, king of the English
14
Edgar Ætheling, brother of
Margaret 4, 22, 25, 32,
34, 35-6, 38, 39, 43-4, 50,
53, 64, 65-71, 76-7, 82, 84

Edith, daughter of
Margaret, *see* Matilda
Edith, wife of Edward the
Confessor 21, 25, 26-7,
30, 31, 34, 48-9, 50, 72
Edmund, son of Margaret
50, 83, 84-5
Edmund, uncle of Margaret
10-11, 13, 18, 21
Edmund II Ironside, king
of the English 9-10, 11,
18, 19, 21, 24, 25, 77
Edward, son of Margaret
50, 79, 80, 81, 82
Edward the Confessor (St),
king of England 3, 20-1,
22, 24, 25, 30, 31, 32, 33,
34, 37, 41, 42-3, 48-9, 50,
55, 83, 84, 97
Edward the Martyr,
king of the English 8
Edward I, king of England
25
Edward Ætheling, father of
Margaret 8, 10-12, 13, 14,
18, 19, 23, 50, 62, 66
Edwin, earl of Mercia 31,
34, 35, 36
Edwin, king of
Northumbria 64
Egelwine, bishop of
Durham 36
Emma of Normandy, wife
of Æthelred II and then
of Cnut 11, 20, 26
Ethelbert, king of Kent 58
Ethelwin, bishop of
Durham 38
Eustace III, count of
Boulogne 85

Florence of Worcester
4, 36, 75
Fothad, Culdee bishop of
St Andrews 58, 78, 85
Francisco de Assisi, king
consort of Spain 97

Gaimar, Geoffrei 11
Géza, Prince, ruler of
Hungary 16, 18
Gillis, Bishop James 96-7
Gisela, countess of
Brunswick 12-13
Gisela, queen of Hungary
13
Godwin, Earl 21, 26, 31
Gondomar, Count of,
Spanish ambassador 91
Gregory, St 28
Gregory I, Pope 58, 61
Gregory VII, Pope 63
Gunnhild, half-sister of
Edward the Confessor
22
Gunnhildr, daughter of
Harold Godwinsson 70
Gyrth, son of Earl Godwin
26, 34
Gytha, wife of Earl Godwin
30, 34

Harald II Hardrada,
king of Norway 5, 32-3,
43
Harold II Godwinsson,
king of England, brother-
in-law of Edward the
Confessor 21, 26, 31, 32,
33-4, 70, 77

Harold I Harefoot, king of
England 20
Harthacnut, king of
England and Denmark
11, 20, 26, 32
Helena, mother of
Constantine the Great
60-1
Henry I, king of England
6, 68, 84, 86, 87
Henry III, king of England
97
Henry VIII, king of
England 25
Henry III, emperor of
Germany 22
Henry IV, emperor of
Germany 22
Henry of Huntingdon, son
of David I 86, 87
Hildegard of Bingen 75
Hole, William 2

Ingegerd, wife of Jaraslow I
11, 12
Ingibiorg, first wife
of Malcolm III 42, 43,
46, 76, 81, 83
Innocent IV, Pope 92
Isabella II, queen of Spain
96-7

James III, king of Scots 91
James VI, of Scotland, and
I, of England 88, 91
James, St, of Compostela
23
Jaraslow I, prince of Kiev
11, 12, 19

Jerome, St 94
Jocelin of Furness 91
John of Fordun 3-4, 36, 45
John of the Cross, St 76
John of Worcester 69
John XII, Pope 16
Joscelin of Canterbury 4

Kenneth MacAlpin,
king of Picts and Scots
41
Knowles, Dom David 84
Koenigsberger, Professor
H. G. 50

Lanfranc, archbishop of
Canterbury 59, 63, 88
Laurence, St 73, 95
Leoba, nun 27-8
Leofwine, son of Earl
Godwin 26, 34
Levente, son of Vászoly 12
Luidolf, margrave of
Westfriesland 12
Lulach, stepson of Macbeth
42, 53, 81

Macbeth, king of Scots 37,
41, 42, 53, 55, 97
MacKenzie, Sir George 95
Mael Snechta, son of
Lulach 53, 81
Maelpedair, mormaer of
Mearns 83
Magnus Barelegs, king of
Norway 85
Magnus, son of Olaf II
12

Malcolm III, king of Scots 2, 4, 5, 6, 17, 33, 36, 37, 39-40, 41-4, 46-7, 49, 50, 51, 52, 53, 54, 55, 58, 60, 62, 64-5, 66-7, 68-71, 72, 73, 76, 77, 78-9, 80, 81-2, 83, 84, 85, 86, 87, 92, 93, 95, 96, 97, 98

Malcolm IV, king of Scots 41

Malcolm, possible son of Malcolm III 42

Malcolm, son of Alexander I 86, 88

Malderus, Bishop John 95

Margaret (St),
  queen of Scots, wife of Malcolm III 4, 5-7, 15, 34-6, 38, 40, 81-4, 85-6, 87, 88, 89, 90; relics of 1, 89, 94-7; images of 1-3, 6, 8; relationship with Malcolm III 2, 46-7, 48, 52, 63, 68, 71, 72, 73, 76, 77, 78-9; marriage 2, 17, 31, 37, 38, 43-4, 45, 46, 49, 52, 58, 64, 66, 76; foundation of church at Dunfermline 4, 49; English ancestry of 8-12, 13-14; birth 13; parentage 13-14, 18-19; in Hungary 18-20, 22, 44; Benedictine influences on 18, 19-20, 26-9, 55, 72-3, 75, 86; journey to England 24; death of father 24; influence of Queen Edith on 25, 26-7, 30; influence of Edward the Confessor on 25-6;

education in England 27-30; relationship with Edgar Ætheling 36, 66-7; arrival in Scotland 36-7; meetings with Malcolm III 37, 39, 41, 44; influence on court life 46, 47-50, 56, 64-5; birth and treatment of children 50, 54, 65, 73, 74, 78, 84, 86; health 53, 73-4, 75-6, 78-9; relations with clergy 55, 58-63; relationship with Lanfranc 59, 63; ecclesiastical councils 60-1; charity 63, 73, 77, 91, 97-8; residence in Edinburgh Castle 64-5; death 75, 77, 78, 80; relationship with Turgot 77-8; religious influence on children 84-5; cult of 88, 91-4, 97-8; canonisation 91, 92-3

Margaret Tudor, wife of James IV 92

Mary, queen of Scots 1, 92, 95

Mary, daughter of Margaret 50, 65, 85

Mary of Guise, wife of James V 92

Matilda (Edith), queen of England, daughter of Margaret 5-6, 49, 50, 51, 52, 65, 69-70, 71, 72, 78, 84, 85, 87

Matilda, granddaughter of Margaret 85

Maxwell, Father Stephen 1

Merleswein, sheriff of Lincoln 35, 36, 38

Merton, Thomas, monk 76

Millais, Sir John Everett 2

Morcar, earl of Mercia 9, 31, 34, 35, 36

Morel, Arkel 79

Mowbray, Robert de, earl of Northumbria 79, 83

Muirchú 89

Nicholas I, Pope 16, 19

Ninian, (St), bishop of the southern Picts 57

Olaf II, king of Norway 11, 12

Olaf III, king of Norway 5

Olaf, king of Sweden 10-11

Orderic Vitalis 14, 32, 34, 37, 69

Orseolo, Ottone, doge of Venice 13

Orseolo, Peter, king of Hungary 13

Oswald, king of Northumbria 57

Otto I, emperor of Germany 16

Otto II, emperor of Germany 16

Otto III, emperor of Germany 17

Paschal II, Pope 60

Paton, Sir Joseph Noel 2

Patrick, St 57, 75, 89

Paul, St 61

Peter, St 26
Philip I, king of France 65
Philip II, king of Spain 95
Photius, patriarch of
  Constantinople 16, 19
Pius IX, Pope 96
Ptolemy, geographer 64

Ritchie, R. L. G. 6, 24, 68,
  73
Robert Curthose, son of
  William I 14, 67, 68, 69,
  70
Robie, John, Jesuit priest
  and missionary 1, 95
Rurik, Norse pirate 12

Samuel Aba, king of
  Hungary 13
Seton, 5th Lord 2
Sibylla, wife of Alexander I
  86
Sicurus, Pope 57
Sigeferth 9
Sinclair, Wendy J. 11
Siward, earl of Northumbria
  35, 41, 42, 55
Skene, W. F. 7
Stephen I, king of England
  85, 87
Stephen (St), king of
  Hungary 8, 12, 13, 14, 16,
  17-18, 85

Stigand, archbishop of
  Canterbury 34
Strachan, Douglas 3
Swein I Forkbeard, king of
  Denmark 9, 38, 39
Sylvester II, Pope 17
Symeon of Durham
  4, 6, 39, 40, 43, 67, 69
Symeon Stylites 75

Taksony, Magyar chief 16
Tennyson, Alfred Lord 2
Teresa of Avila, St 76
Teresa, Mother 17
Thérèse of Lisieux, (St) 76
Thomas of Celano 56
Tirechán 89
Tostig, son of Earl Godwin
  26, 31-3, 37, 43
Turgot, prior of Durham,
  bishop of St Andrews 4-
  7, 8, 24, 28, 40, 45-6, 47,
  49, 51, 53, 55, 58-9, 61, 62,
  63, 71, 72, 74, 75, 77-8,
  79, 84, 86, 89, 90-1, 98

Ulster Cycle 67

Vászoly of Hungary 12, 13,
  17, 85
Vianney, St Jean-Baptiste-
  Marie 75

Vladimir, prince of Kiev 19

Walcher, bishop of Durham
  6
Walgar, Earl 11
Waltheof, son of Earl
  Siward 35, 38
Wenceslas, duke of Bohemia
  23
Wilfrid, (St), bishop of
  Hexham 58
William, son of Duncan II
  82, 84
William I, the Lion, king of
  Scots 92
William I, the Conqueror,
  duke of Normandy and
  king of England 4, 6, 14,
  21, 32, 33-4, 35, 36, 38-9,
  44, 52, 53, 59, 65-6, 67,
  68, 69, 72, 77, 97
William of Calais, bishop
  of Durham 71
William of Malmesbury 4,
  9, 10, 11, 32, 67, 69, 71,
  84
William of Poitiers 35
William Rufus, king of
  England 68-71, 78-9, 82,
  83-4, 86
Wilson, Alan J. 11, 21, 38

Mary of Guise
Rosalind K Marshall
Scots' Lives series

Mary of Guise tells the story of an inspirational leader, the mother of Mary, queen of Scots. This intelligent young Frenchwoman came to believe that it was her mission to bring order, peace and justice to Scotland, regardless of personal cost. A subtle politician and staunch Roman Catholic, she was to earn the respect of her contemporaries and most Scottish historians ever since for her determination and courage. Written by an expert on 16th- and 17th-century Scottish history and based on original 16th-century French and Scottish documents, the descriptive narrative brings this remarkable queen of Scots to life.

ISBN 1 901663 63 9/£6.99

Phoebe Anna Traquair 1852-1936
Elizabeth Cumming
co-publication with the
National Galleries of Scotland

Phoebe Anna Traquair occupies a unique position within British art. She was Scotland's first significant woman artist of the modern age and a valued contributor to the British Arts and Crafts movement. Seventy years after her death, her murals are treasured and her crafts – embroidery, manuscript illumination, bookbinding, enamelwork, furniture decoration and easel painting – are in demand among collectors. The book has many beautiful colour illustrations including artworks not previously published, and quotations from Traquair's private letters.

ISBN 1 901663 98 1/£9.95

Churches to Visit in Scotland
Scotland's Churches Scheme

The fourth edition of this indispensable guide describes 1,001 places of worship across the denominations in Scotland (Church of Scotland, Roman Catholic, Scottish Episcopal, Free Church, Baptist, Methodist, United Reformed, Greek Orthodox and Jewish) and includes the history and architectural details of each building, times of services, access, location details, map references, and availability of refreshments and souvenirs. Most of the buildings are shown in specially commissioned line drawings.

ISBN 1 905267 00 2/c.£8.99

The Skating Minister
Duncan Thomson and
Lynne Gladstone-Millar
co-publication with the
National Galleries of Scotland

The portrait of the Reverend Robert Walker by Sir Henry Raeburn is world famous. On permanent show in the National Gallery of Scotland, the black-clad minister, skating enigmatically over Edinburgh's Duddingston Loch on a wintry afternoon, has become a familiar icon of Scottish culture. The book explores the relationship between artist and sitter, the times they lived in and the reasons why the portrait has acquired such iconic status.

ISBN 1 901663 85 X/£9.95

Reginald Johnston

Shiona Airlie

Scots' Lives series

Born in Edinburgh, Reginald Johnston entered the colonial service and became a district officer in China where he explored, studied the language and culture, and adopted Buddhism. In 1919 he met the thirteen year-old Emperor Puyi for the first time. Johnston was often thought by his contemporaries to be strange, difficult and eccentric, but he knew how to capture a child's imagination and quickly gained Puyi's trust and friendship. The Scot was the only foreigner working in the Forbidden City, and Puyi appointed him Mandarin of the highest rank. This is the first complete biography of the man who was both explorer and writer; and who history will remember as tutor and advisor to the last Emperor of China.

ISBN 1 901663 49 3/£6.99

Romanesque and Gothic Decorative Metalwork and Ivory Carvings in the Museum of Scotland

Virginia Glenn

The metalwork and ivory carvings depicted in this important book cover the 12th to 16th centuries, illustrating Scotland's history at a key period, when the nation was emerging as an independent entity with links across Europe. As we might expect, many different styles of church decoration are included – in the collection of seal matrices alone, we see outstanding carving on the seal of Brechin Cathedral and childlike crudity on that of the burgh of Arbroath. The NMS collection of decorative metalwork and ivory carvings also includes some of the world-famous Lewis chess pieces, the Whithorn and St Fillan's croziers, the Guthrie Bell Shrine, Bute Mazer, and many outstanding examples of gold and silver jewellery.

ISBN 1 901663 558/£35.00

TO FIND OUT MORE ABOUT BOOKS AVAILABLE FROM THE NATIONAL MUSEUMS OF SCOTLAND, CONTACT:

NMS Enterprises Limited – Publishing
National Museums of Scotland
Chambers Street
Edinburgh EH1 1JF